MODERN TIMES

responding to chaos

drawings and films
selected by Lutz Becker

Lutz Becker
Nick Wadley
David Elliott
Iain Boyd Whyte

Kettle's Yard, University of Cambridge

published to accompany an exhibition shown at:
Kettle's Yard, Cambridge ▪ 16 January - 14 March 2010
De La Warr Pavilion, Bexhill-on-Sea ▪ 1 April - 13 June 2010

designed by Paul Allitt, printed by C3imaging, Colchester

ISBN 978 1 904561 36 1

This and other Kettle's Yard publications are available from
Kettle's Yard, Castle Street, Cambridge, CB3 0AQ
telephone 01223 748100 ▪ www.kettlesyard.cam.ac.uk

cover: 76. Richard Serra (b.1939), **Tracks # 46**, 2008 © ARS, NY and DACS, London 2010

right: 68. Liubov Popova (1889-1924), **Spatial Force Construction**, 1921

Foreword

'Modern Times' is conceived as a series of exhibitions where we invite creative individuals to trace their own paths through the twentieth and twenty-first centuries, the idea being that, exhibition by exhibition, the series will build an informal, accumulating history of the art of our times.

Ten years into the twenty-first century one thing is clear: that there can be no single history of the art of the last hundred years. It is the period into which we were born and the timing and geography of our birth have much to do with how we see it.

Lutz Becker, the author of this first exhibition, was brought up in East Berlin between the ruins of the Second World War and the tensions of the Cold War. The family transferred to West Berlin in 1955, his father, a liberal politician, having returned from imprisonment in Siberia under the Communist regime. From studentship at the Slade School of Fine Art, under William Coldstream and film director Thorold Dickinson, he emerged into 1960s London, publicly as a film-maker on art and politics, more privately as an abstract painter.

'Modern Times' is also seen as an umbrella for other voices to come together. Here Lutz Becker is joined by art historian Nick Wadley, museum curator David Elliott and architectural historian Iain Boyd Whyte, each reflecting on notions of modernity. And, during the exhibition, programmes of film, music, lectures and discussion will broaden the exploration.

It is particularly apt that an exhibition such as this should bring together two of the iconic buildings and institutions of modern times in this country: Erich Mendelsohn and Serge Chermayeff's architectural gem, the De la Warr Pavilion in Bexhill, and Jim Ede's model of collecting art and creating rooms, Kettle's Yard in Cambridge.

Michael Harrison
Director, Kettle's Yard

Alan Haydon
Director, De La Warr Pavilion

Contents

Introduction

Lutz Becker

… All artistic movements, whether consciously or not, seek the destruction of traditional aesthetic worlds, the reduction of 'forms' to elementary germinal, embryonic states, in the hope of creating 'fresh worlds', or in other words, of abolishing the history of art and re-living the dawning moment when man saw the world for the first time.

Mircea Eliade: *La nostalgie des origines*, 1969

Drawings are traces of time and thought. It is the awareness of time as the measure of the distance between thought and realisation, of the value of the transient and sense of the fragility of the inspirational moment that made me decide to show in this exhibition predominantly works on paper. It may not be a complete appraisal of modern and contemporary drawing but I attempt to explore the challenges that artists faced and are still facing in the pursuit of abstraction, non-objectivity and the conceptual extension of the medium itself. Drawing is no longer, as it was in previous epochs, about the recording of reality and appearance alone. Drawing is for the contemporary artist the most accessible terrain for experimentation – an expression of freedom. It is a daring, independent medium reflecting its own becoming. Process and material are often the subject /object of the work itself.

27. Raimund Girke (1930-2002) , **Untitled**, 1998

Some of the most important modern artists use drawing – the oldest and most fundamental art – to explore and re-assess problems of form, space and time. Drawing was and is about mark making with pencil, graphite, charcoal or chalk, with pen, brush and ink, to record traces of mental and physical energy. Paul Klee defines in his *Pedagogical Sketchbook* the act of drawing as an act of intuition: 'An active line which moves freely; a walk for a walk's sake, without aim.'[1] The hand sketches and hatches. Its movements inscribe seismographic changes of pressure on the paper in the form of lines, dots, scriptural quivers. The materiality and presence of a drawing is dependent on the type or quality of paper used. Fibre and grain structure, thickness, weight, tone and the finish of the paper influence the character of a drawing, of how graphite or ink stand on the surface or are absorbed, and how, in the end, substance and light interact.

Shifts in line, form, association and temperament can be found, like in the words and verses of poets, in the lines of draughtsmen and women. Like poetry, drawing is a highly sensitive medium, often open-ended, full of possibilities. Drawings explore, reflect and re-confirm visual concepts and ideas. Traces, marks, erasures on paper, sometimes hesitant, sometimes performed with the intensity of scorch-marks, are the foremost means for testing them. New kinds of representation and measured degrees of abstraction alter and extend the range of the artist's as well as the viewer's perception and critical perspective. Artists in search of truly contemporary solutions develop a fierce opposition against any form of convention. They unlearn, wilfully or subconsciously, established skills and learn new ways by breaking the boundaries of their chosen media. Artists question traditional notions, either through transforming them or by discarding them. Jodi Hauptman summarised these processes aptly: 'It is in drawing's intimate laboratory – in the erasing, and smudging, tearing and pasting – that we can see most clearly…the ways in which artists negotiate opposing terms, ideals, and beliefs.'[2] Art has become self-conscious. The quest for originality and authenticity has been dramatically extended through the interaction of art and technology, particularly the inclusion of photography, film and video. The discovery of useful links and dependencies between these media and experimental art are a source of dialogue and inspiration. The principle of self-critical exploration has opened a range of creative strategies to artists who generalise and utilise the prevailing condition of alienation. A new rationalism has become the basis for a generation of conceptualists and minimalists.

Encompassing the twentieth and twenty-first centuries, the works in this exhibition are presented in a non-chronological order to explore contrasts, internal connections and conceptual affinities as they emerge in the work of artists separated by time and geography. The exhibition comprises works by some key artists from Europe and America; the selection also includes works of contemporary artists who are less known and others who have been sidelined in the unpredictable stream of modern art history.

footnotes

1   Paul Klee, *Pädagogisches Skizzenbuch*, Bauhausbuch No.2, ed. Walter Gropius and László Moholy-Nagy, Munich 1925 p.1.1

2   Jody Hauptman, 'Imagination without Strings', in *Drawing from the Modern*, 1880-1945, New York, 2004 p.52

8

58. Piet Mondrian (1872-1944), **Tree Study**, early 1913

11. Karoline Bröckel (b.1964), **Snow / Werkgruppe Schnee**, 2006

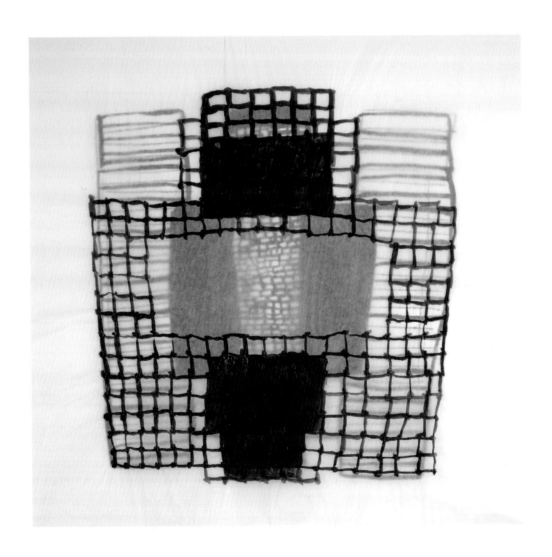

32. Susan Hefuna (b. 1962), Building, 2009

DRAWING AND DRAWINGS

Nick Wadley

Richard Serra said in an interview once that he could imagine nothing, in any of the arts, that was so autobiographically direct as a drawing. An artist's drawing is a form of his or her handwriting, and as susceptible to graphology. Serra called it 'the most credible indication of who people are'. As a sentiment this finds echoes in the writing and statements of many modern artists, maybe most. And it is more than the old cliché that drawing lets us closer to the artist than anything else. It is as though, in modern times, this subjective role has somehow become a meaning or function of drawing.

Nothing, for instance, could give a more complete account of Giacometti and the way he thought than a drawing by him. His idea was to make an image of visual sensations, less about forms in space than about his sensations of a fluctuating relationship between form and space. He evolved an exacting manner of drawing that is nevertheless full of suggestion and equivocation: an art – in David Sylvester's apt phrase – 'that is tentative but is not vague'. Giacometti said once that of the two tools of the draughtsman, the pencil and the rubber, he wasn't sure which was the more important. The lifespan of a drawing by him was of an image being continually revised and reduced, sometimes so repeatedly erased and redrawn that the surface of the paper was exhausted. It was a process likened to the writing of Beckett, his friend, as a celebration of the inconclusive. It is true that Giacometti drew some perverse pleasure from the impossibility of what he sought, but his was an ironic not a pessimistic pleasure.

Giacometti's working life spans the middle-ground of the 'modern times' covered by this exhibition and, in its abiding concern with images of things seen, his drawn oeuvre may seem to belong more with earlier traditions of representation than with the currents of subjectivity and abstractness which define most drawing today. However, the early history of this modern abstract drawing also involved images of sensation and fugitive experience.

Alberto Giacometti (1901-1966), Elizabeth – **head and shoulders**, 1955
pencil on paper, (not in exhibition)
Robert and Lisa Sainsbury Collection, University of East Anglia
© ADAGP/FAAG, Paris and DACS, London 2010

styles of drawing that were thrust upon them in the life-rooms and cast-rooms of their student days. But their main quests were less self-consciously to do with radical technique *per se*, than with their wish for an art that was of and about sensations of the real world and modern life. This led to new subjects – transient, often fragmentary images of movement and change, which required new means. It was sometimes just a matter of speed – finish, detail and style were sacrificed to the urgency of capturing something in movement, or a fleeting ensemble. The act of seeing became their subject, as much as the thing seen. And in the process, their drawing descended into an incoherence of image that was outrageous to contemporary eyes. This in its turn emancipated marks on paper or canvas as abstract forms, giving rise to a new ('abstract') coherence. It is at the heart of what Clement Greenberg in his mandarin-like way later termed 'area' drawing (as distinct from 'sculptural' drawing, which was 'finicking and petty'). He was writing around 1960, discussing an influential revival of interest among American painters in the 'silted-up space' of late Monet.

beginnings of modern times

It was within the impressionist and symbolist art of the late nineteenth century that a critical break with conventions of representation first showed its hand. Of course there were presentiments in the drawing of their mentors, the giants of Romanticism earlier in the century: Goya, Delacroix, Daumier. But it is in the inherently subjective nature of an 'impression', and in the urgently, artlessly-made marks – more felt than reasoned – by which the impression is expressed, that a crude, new-born graphic art became visible.

When Impressionism took drawing to this edge, this moment of crisis, it was almost despite itself. It is true that the impressionists deplored what seemed to them formulaic

This historical leapfrog from the avant-garde of the 1860s-80s to the modernism of the 1950s-70s, and between old Europe and new America is a very telling connection in the lineage of the modern drawing, where there has often been more talk of difference than of descent. It also throws up some hints about the relative roles of Impressionism/Symbolism on the one hand, and Cézanne/Cubism on the other, in the evolution of the abstract modern drawing.

The most explicit influence of Impressionism on early modern drawing came from impressionist painting, from the exposed fragmentation of its painted surface. The array of separate brush-marks through which they realised all of their transient effects of light and colour and their

Georges Seurat, **Standing Woman in Profile (Promenade)**, c.1882/87
pen and ink, 29.8 x 23.4 cm (not in exhibition)
Von der Heydt Museum, Wuppertal

precocious instant-likenesses of town and country, had a relatively short life as an avant-garde idiom. And in the field of drawing, when the *rappel à l'ordre* of the 1880s came, the techniques of the great draughtsmen of post-Impressionism were largely founded in a reconfiguration of this abandoned array of small units. This is most obvious in the homogeneous pointillist fabrics of neo-Impressionism.

Van Gogh's experimental textured drawings in Paris and Arles that led to the spectacular reed-pen techniques of his brief maturity were knowingly crafted out of impressionist brush-marks. The dense inner life of Seurat's graphic work was born from a strange mongrel fusion of the animated impressionist surface with aspects of academic drawing. And in Cézanne's art, we can watch impressionist marks being steadily nurtured through hatched pencil and chalk notations in his sketchbooks, into the refined harmonies of contrast and analogy, in drawn and coloured marks, of his late watercolours. The relation between these and the crystalline, small-unit structures of Cubism and Futurism is part of history, and a route from there to the high formalist modernism in Holland and Russia around the First World War is the most familiar account of the origins of Abstract Art.

Henry van de Velde's austere but lyrical drawing *Sea and Beach* gives a good account of the impressionist chrysalis transforming into a modernist butterfly. Marks whose origins lay in a rendering of land, water and sky become musical notations of an abstract poem.

When in the later twentieth century American artists sought to distinguish the autonomy of their abstract drawing from old European practices, it is a post-impressionist/cubist genre of constructed relationships that they had in mind (remember Greenberg's disparaging reference

to 'sculptural' drawing). Comments by many artists (Stella, Judd, for instance) confirm that it was a European aesthetic of geometric relationships and the juxtaposition of parts that felt irrelevant and alien to them. Barnett Newman recognised an abstract 'reality of transcendent experience' in American art that was something quite distinct from inherent concerns in European modernism with the 'transcendence of objects' (1947). Other colour field painters felt estranged from drawing's properties of edge and of surface, as antipathetic to stained colour. But much of the discussion surrounding drawing was a matter of semantics, and many American artists still saw painting and drawing as inseparable. Drawing was either a way of beginning – 'a way of tuning your perception' (Serra), or a part of all art – 'just the handling of material is an aspect of drawing' (Noland). Rauschenberg and Johns used drawing like anything else in their art. A bit of drawing was like any other 'stuff' or any other object. In the 1960s Rauschenberg experimented with the erasure of drawings (including, famously, a de Kooning) in the pursuit of 'whiteness'. Johns uses an area of graphite hatching in his work in the same physical way as a stencilled word or a painted image or a

Henry van der Velde, **Sea and beach**, 1888/89
black chalk, 23 x 31 cm (not in exhibition)
Private Collection, Amsterdam

modern times

Maybe, anyway, drawing over the last hundred years has outgrown all historical polemics? The enormously broad canvas of Lutz Becker's selection of works for this exhibition suggests as much. Drawing in modern times has come of age as a medium, commanding its own sovereign terms of reference. There are no significant distinctions to be made in this world between abstraction and representation, or between 'the abstract' and 'the object', since the object lives its abstract life alongside anything and everything else. The spirit of Kurt Schwitters' exuberant discovery, as early as 1919, that he could draw with lines, words, collage, cartoon-like pictures, rubber stamps and whatever else he happened upon runs through the whole show.

In this sense the exhibition not only affirms the enormous variety of forms taken by drawing, but also reveals along the way sensibilities that are common to the practice of drawing, however different those who draw, and where or whenever they drew. The range is from the celebrated to the little-known, and from the near-caricatural, the rough-hewn and the expressionist to the minimalist, the musical and the conceptual. We find a Seurat-like sensuality in the austere graphite geometry of Alan Reynolds' untitled drawing (2004), the drifting lines of Raimund Girke (1998), and in the heraldic carnival of Léger's *Trees* (1923). The impish energy of airborne elements in a tiny suprematist drawing by Malevich (1916) is shared with the amoeba-like creatures and fingerprints that float through a Lucebert dream (1962). Similar semaphores in space echo between abstract forms in charcoal and gouache by Joel Shapiro (1994) and a gesticulating, multi-headed figure in ink and wash by Franciszka Themerson (1972). The same wide world of graphic notation is shared by works as different as the eyes-closed, two-handed *Subway* drawings of Anastasi

nailed-on tin can. 'Take an object, do something to it, do something else to it.' Drawing is one of those objects.

One final point of history. There was another channel in abstract art's early history that had little to do with either cubist relationships or the object. This connects the sensations of Impressionism directly, through the expressive abstraction of Symbolism and of Art Nouveau, with the early abstract painting of Kandinsky. Like the symbolists, the young Kandinsky recognised a musical dimension in Monet's impressions, as a liberating spirit. And in Art Nouveau circles, exploiting the unprejudiced world of the applied arts, the vital life of the drawn line was celebrated for its own organic energies. Maybe this thread has a more lasting relevance to the whole gamut of modern drawing?

Kurt Schwitters, **Druchsache**, c. 1919
chalk, collage, rubber stamp, 23 x 18 cm (not in exhibition)
Sprengel Museum, Hanover © DACS 2010

(1967), products equally of concept and chance, and the delicate plotted webs of Susan Hefuna (2008), which she likens to building a house. Visitors to the exhibition will be seduced by the selection and the hanging into finding their own personal analogies, and surprises.

One of the surprises that drawing may offer is a glimpse behind the public façade of an artist's work. I have long suspected that inside each highly formal artist is someone else trying to get out, and I value glimpses of an alter ego in the wit and irony to be found in notebooks or informal works by the makers of very straight-faced, minimalist art. Seeing a faintly comic work once by Dan Flavin, a crude yellow box with a yellow domestic light-bulb on top, helped me to appeciate the life of his neon tubes differently. And the example exhibited here from among his many drawings of sailboats may prompt another sort of new thought about his work at large.

Our knowledge of Ad Reinhardt's ironic cartoons about art always lurks meaningfully behind the ascetic black rectangles of his painting. The prolific early career of Lyonel Feininger as cartoonist/illustrator, on the other hand, may come as a surprise to those familiar only with his svelte geometric painting and drawing of spacious skies and seas. In the event, not only did the inventive graphic facility of his first career equip him well for the improvised abstraction of Cubism, but the element of gothic fantasy that abounds in that precocious early oeuvre remained meaningful in the private iconography of a lifetime of drawing. Intermittently among his more private drawings, there appear strange spiky figures, like *Seven Mannikins* of 1954. Feininger sometimes referred to them as 'ghosties', and although their true role is never revealed, it seems likely that they represented some form of private demon, skeletons in his psychological cupboard.

high art and low art

Moments of proximity in drawing between 'low art' and 'high art' are as striking as the distance at which the two are held apart and segregated by established artistic convention and practice at large. Even in so pluralist and liberal-minded an exhibition as this, there is no place for such masters of drawing from the popular domain as Saul Steinberg or Roland Topor or Quino or Tomi Ungerer or Sempé, nor any surprise that this should be so. But outside, in the real world, these artists and others like them have exerted enormous influence over our education in the art of the line. At a fair of architecture and design once, in Milan in 1954, Steinberg drew a line along the wall that was thirty three feet long. It transformed itself (and the wall) continually throughout its length, in and out of gravity – from line to sea, to string, to road, to writing, to floor, to rooftops, to sky, and back to line again.

Saul Steinberg (1914-1999), **Untitled**, 1948
ink on paper, 36 x 29 cm (not in exhibition)
Beinicke Rare Book and Manuscript Library, Yale University
© The Saul Steinberg Foundation/ARS, NY and DACS, London 2010

There were a few instances earlier in the twentieth century of popular or 'vulgar' manners of drawing or image being imported into 'Fine Art' (posters and other print media around Art Nouveau; cubist and dada collages). But the most significant and seminal breach was made in the 1960s, most obviously within Pop Art and various new forms of realist painting, and the inroads they made into the fortress of high formalist art. In 1961 Jean Dubuffet, another who dabbled in a cartoon-like manner of drawing, spoke of his lifetime in art spent in constant fluctuation between a bias towards *personnages'* and a bias against them. The art of Philip Guston at around this date was vacillating around the same issue, his abstract expressionist drawings and paintings increasingly animated by a latent figuration. When he remade his art in the late 1960s, he brought all the scale of his early murals and the sensual handling of his abstract paintings to bear on the simplest of graphic images. He wrote '…in front of the canvas or the drawing paper, I feel like an innocent – a beginner – a primitive.' Such a phrase might prepare us for the originality of the later drawing, but not for its monumental aplomb.

The highly formed language of late Guston drawing reflects the strip-cartoon graphic culture in which he grew up. The status of the comic strip and cartoon carried more weight in American culture than in Europe (cartoon art has on occasion been exhibited in New York as art, with other art), and Guston, like his peers an avid follower of 'the funnies' as an adolescent, had also toyed briefly with a career as cartoonist. A striking coincidence of image and manner in 1967/68 between drawings by Guston and cartoons by Robert Crumb was even discussed in terms of influence, but it seems to have been just coincidence, their common heritage in US comic artists. This confrontational 'lowness' of Guston's new drawing dramatised his departure from the abstract-expressionist fold, and presented itself as a

stand for engaged subject matter. His drawing had moved out of abstractions into an enormously graspable and grasping world. It has other hallmarks of comic-strip art, too. His repetitions, and his more-or-less recognisable cast of characters almost build up a narrative continuity. All that would be needed to complete the cartoon repertory are captions and a drawn frame. In practice, words and frames are not uncommon in modern drawing. They are made with the same lines.

lines on paper

I likened drawing to handwriting earlier on. Letters are also linear graphic devices, no less an invention of man, and often drawn with the same tool. Van Gogh wrote his letters with the same pen as he used to make most of the drawings he enclosed with them. I have wondered whether his easy fluency with the pen as an artist wasn't in part born from his prolific letter-writing. Since the days of typography's frequent appearance in cubist, futurist and dada drawings and collages, the written word has become a natural part of drawing's graphic language, in Cy Twombly for instance. And by the same token drawing has shown predilections for calligraphic forms (Michaux, Tobey, Afnan), sometimes under the influence of oriental art. (Picasso mused once that if he'd been born Chinese he would have written his pictures.) Writing makes several appearances in the course of this exhibition – words among the lines, and lines that behave like a script across the paper. Title and signature can also play a significant role in the forms and composition of a drawing.

Until the first mark is made, each sheet of white paper is a virgin, sovereign territory, as empty and as infinite as the sky. At the end of his life, Matisse described the luminous space of his white paper, and spoke of his line 'modelling its light'. Each line stakes its claim for a position in the sovereign space. Its location on the paper is certain, but its location in this space remains as ambiguous spatially as a distant star in an empty sky, until and unless the addition of further lines and marks sets up a coherent configuration.

One thing that distinguishes the modern drawing is that these two locations of each mark — on the flat paper and in pictorial space — are equally exposed. The paper is never a neutral ground. It is an active part of the drawing. With a very few, mainly early exceptions this is true of all the drawings exhibited here. And in this context, when — as in Karoline Bröckel's sensitively observed *Snow* (2006) — a title suddenly invites us into a figurative spatial reading of the marks on paper, it comes almost as a shock.

A drawn frame, within the rectangle of a drawing is also just lines, like any others. In traditional drawings we could reasonably assume that a boundary line drawn around a drawing suggested a completed state, like the frame around a picture on the wall. Many sketchbook scribbles, over the centuries, have rough framing lines around a part of the page, isolating a motif to be painted.

In a modern drawing the framing line often acts quite differently, simply as the separation of space inside the frame from a margin of the same space left outside. The frame is part of the drawing, so is the margin. I first recognised this difference in the pages of an album of drawings in which Goya had drawn a brush line (sometimes double) around each image. The effect is to conjure a window or doorway in the paper, through which you step to take part in the magical other world of pictorial space. It is a practice that Giacometti adopted increasingly in drawings, and, especially, in his portrait paintings (which are effectively brush drawings). It's not clear when he drew the framing lines; certainly they weren't the last lines to

be drawn and were perhaps even made quite early in the process, staking out the pictorial territory. He often draws two frames, one inside another, as if refining or intensifying the space within which he might realise his dream — the sensation of a gaze.

There is a good instance of this device in the exhibition, in a pastel by Victor Willing, one of a remarkable series he drew around 1980. The agitated motifs resemble still life objects that appear disturbed or possessed by an inner life — they almost behave like figures. The motif is set up in a rapid charcoal drawing, including a drawn frame. His pastel reworking of the image, in saturated colour, often bulges into the margins. It is very physical, carrying a strong sense of its making and of the artist's presence in the

Goya, **Philosophy goes barefoot and in rags** (Petrarch), c.1820
brush and indian ink. 26.6 x 18.2 cm (not in exhibition)
Private Collection

smudges or finger marks that accompany his signature, date, and sometimes a title, in the margin. Many of these pastels were enlarged quite exactly into paintings, but none of the paintings has a drawn frame, so the motif occupies the whole canvas, right out to the edges. The difference is striking.

In the drawings, the unequivocal effect of the frame is to emphasise the imaginary world of the picture, without pretence, as marks on paper. The image is offered like a bit of magic on a tray. You are invited through the frame onto its stage, like Alice through the looking glass, and with no attempt to disguise the drawn artifice of it all. 'I am just a drawing', it says, as you step inside.

This exposed physical life of the marks is probably what all of the very different works in this exhibition have most in common. We feel close to drawing and respond to its signals, known and unknown, partly because we all make lines one way or another – the line is a democratic lingua franca that touches the unconscious – and partly because this exposed immediacy of the marks on the paper carries in it so much of the individual artist, the touch, the mood, even the duration of the drawing. As Serra says, a drawing offers very direct access to its maker.

For most artists, drawing is a part of life, something they do every day, from childhood onwards, as natural and as necessary as dreaming.

references

Richard Serra is quoted from an interview with Judith Wechsler in her film, *Drawing, The Thinking Hand*, Musée du Louvre, Paris 1996.

David Sylvester is quoted from *Looking at Giacometti*, London 1996.

Clement Greenberg is quoted from 'The Later Monet' (1955/59). *Art & Culture*, London 1973, p.45.

Barnett Newman is quoted from a letter to The Nation, N.Y., Dec 1947, cited in Thomas B Hess, *Barnett Newman*, N.Y. 1969.

Kenneth Noland (n.d.) is cited in Barbara Rose, *The American Artist Speaks*, vol II, N.Y. 1981, p.98.

Philip Guston is quoted from a letter of 13 Nov 1975, cited by Michael Auping in *Philip Guston Retrospective*, London 2004, p.20.

Matisse is quoted from 'Notes of a Painter on his Drawing', 1939, translated in Jack D Flam, *Matisse on Art*, London 1973, p.81.

Other comments by artists quoted here, directly or indirectly, have been remembered without a note of their source.

46. Fernand Léger (1881-1977), *Trees*, 1923

12. Carlo Carra (1881-1966), *Synthesis of a Café Concert*, 1910/12

3. Frank Auerbach (b.1931), **Tree at Tretire**, 1975

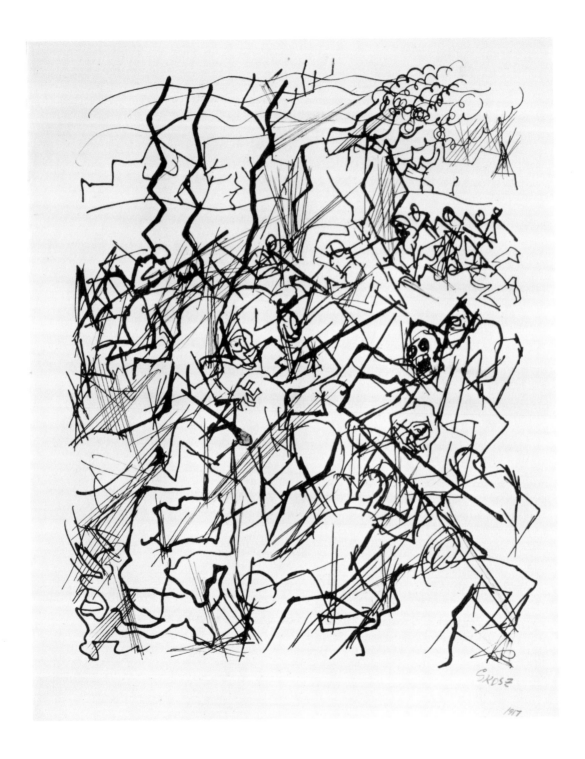

30. George Grosz (1893-1959), War Drawing, 1917

50. Lucebert (Lubertus J. Swaanswijk) (1924-1994), **Untitled**, 1962

16. Otto Dix (1891-1969), Klage (Lament), 1915

20. Lothar Fischer (1933-2004), Untitled, c1970
© DACS 2010

25. William Gear (1915-1997), **Feature in Landscape**, 1948

65. Eduardo Paolozzi (1924-2005), **London Zoo Aquarium**, 1951

79. Louis Soutter (1871-1942), **Errant toujours, les Juifs** (Always wandering, the Jews), 1930/37

45. Michail Larionov (1881-1964), **White Drawing**, 1907 © ADAGP, Paris and DACS, London 2010

8. David Bomberg (1890-1957), **Cubist Composition of Figures**, c.1912/13 © The artists' family

4. Andrés Belmar (b.1966), **Untitled**, 2009

60. Zoran Music (1909-2005), **Four heads with curly hair**, 1973

26. Alberto Giacometti (1901-1966), **The Skull**, 1923
© ADAGP/FAAG, Paris and DACS, London 2009

10. Stuart Brisley (b.1933), **Pig Wars**, 2008

63. Claes Oldenburg (b. 1929), **The Colossal Soap Seen from the Riverbank** in Moonlight-Going, 1991

34

36. Rachel Howard (b.1969), **Untitled Drawing 5**, 2007
Photo Prudence Cuming Associates / Courtesy Murderme

44. Willem de Kooning (1904-1997), **Untitled**, 1966/67
© The Willem de Kooning Foundation, New York/ ARS, NY and DACS, London 2010

81. Friedemann von Stockhausen (b.1945), **Head**, 1988

The Age of Modernisms

Lutz Becker

1.

The art of the twentieth century and of our time is distinctly urban, largely uninvolved in the contemplation of nature. The city, the place where mankind re-invents itself, is the milieu in which most contemporary artists study, work and find their inspiration. The asymmetries of urban life provide the contrasts, contradictions and conflicts, the sparking points for most artistic discoveries and advances.

Modernist tendencies emerged first in the art of the impressionists and symbolists. Their creative conflict with naturalism lay at the roots of Cubism and Futurism. Both -isms emerged virtually simultaneously in France and Italy. The cubist impulse, exemplified in the works of George Braque and Pablo Picasso, addressed immediate problems of pictorial representation and generated theoretical discussions affecting the future interpretation of plasticity and figuration. Cubism paved the way that would eventually lead towards abstraction. Futurism adopted the aesthetics of industry and engineering, of speed, dynamism and electrification. The Futurists, led by F.T. Marinetti, wanted to revolutionise all the arts, believing that innovation and progress could only be promoted through provocative intervention. Their universal ambition was expressed most eloquently in the bold language of their manifestos, calls for artistic, and at times, political actions. These manifestos and propositions were the precursors of a theoretical and practical experimentalism which was the precursor of the now common notion of art as concept.

While the belief of the early modernists was still shaped by the positivistic expectation of the previous century, of stability and the universality of meaning, the ground shifted dramatically with the Great War. This war had been anticipated with fear and forebodings, but was eventually accepted as an inevitable station in Europe's destiny, as the source of radical change and revolution. It was the cataclysmic event that separated the modern world from the historical continuities of the past. The collapse of the old structures left behind a sense of loss and displacement. It fell to the artist to interpret and reflect on the tension and fractures that had emerged in society, by creating concepts and a new visual language that could interact with and utilise the staccato of discontinuity.

The inventions of the Cubists and Futurists, their ability to perceive and describe simultaneity and the parallelism of opposites had shaped the self-awareness and practical capacities of the artists returning from the war. In Switzerland and Germany dadaist actions and provocative passion broke old moulds; the pendulum swung from art to anti-art and back. Richard Huelsenbeck, member of the Berlin Dada group, stated in 1918: 'The best artists will be those who every hour snatch the tatters of their bodies out of the frenzied cataract of life, who, with bleeding hands and hearts, hold fast to the intelligence of their time.'[1] The pathos of these words expressed a kind of apocalyptic *Sturm und Drang*. Faced by the rawness of post-war experience it seemed strangely applicable to both the

Dadaists, destroyers of convention and style, and the romantic emotionalism of the Expressionists.

Revolution gave artists new energies and the psychological robustness to deal with the prevailing condition of chaos. New ideological platforms changed the context of art. For the first time art entered the city streets and became a matter of wider public interest. The experience of war and revolution had sensitised the public and prepared it to shed prejudices and mental routines and promoted an understanding of the new art based on collage, montage, construction and abstraction. The dynamism of the expanding cities, the growth of industry, the attractions of the new functional architecture of concrete and glass and modern design gave tangible proof of progress. Architects defined in their works not only the social ambitions of their time but gave outline and certainty to a collective vision of the future. Modern art and architecture were considered forward-looking, hopeful and positive; in this cultural climate novelty became accepted as an artistic criterion.

In Italy the Futurists supported the Fascist revolution of Mussolini. The 1915 manifesto *The Futurist Reconstruction of the Universe* signed by Balla and Depero was to mark a new beginning.[2] It transcended aesthetics and penetrated the social sphere; art was to define reality. It was a functional manifesto that advocated intervention at all levels and a total fusion of art and life. Italian art and architecture developed under Mussolini in a climate swaying between progress and regression, exemplified in rationalist architecture and design, the toleration of abstraction in the arts and, in contrast, the historicism and *novecento* mentality of the later 1930s. Fascism eventually usurped the modernising energy of the Futurists, a fact that undermined Futurism's effectiveness as an art movement and overshadowed its historical reputation for years to come.

Already, before the war, Russia had had its own independent group of Futurists. In the belief that this was their opportunity to participate in the total renewal of society, they enthusiastically joined the Bolshevik Revolution. There emerged in Moscow and Leningrad a new group of artists: the Constructivists. In their pursuit of a wider collective impact these artists politicised their role by taking 'art to the people'. Revolutionary artists like Alexandr Rodchenko, Gustav Klucis, Aleksei Gan, El Lissitzky and others perceived the creative act as an act of organisation of material and technical capacities. For the first time women artists joined the avant-garde: Liubov Popova, Olga Rosanova and Varvara Stepanova became role models for a generation of independent, creative, modern women. They too taught at the Moscow VKhUTEMAS, the Higher State Artistic and Technical Studios, centre for interdisciplinary experimentation in the fields of painting, sculpture, architecture and design. The aim was to eliminate the hitherto existing division between art and industrial production. With intuitive logic and the precision of engineers the Constructivists bridged the tension between analysis and synthesis, finding concepts that led them towards new systems of art production and practical application. The relationship of the act of making and the enhancement of material qualities, defined as *factura*, added unexpected spiritual values to their materialist ideology. Geometric abstraction, construction and production possessed utopian dimensions. After Lenin's death and Stalin's rise to power Soviet avant-gardists, denounced as formalists, had their creative basis eroded; many of the artists were forbidden to continue working, even suffered deportation to Siberia. With the introduction of the doctrine of Socialist Realism in 1932 the revolution had finally betrayed its avant-garde. Stalin was intent on transforming artists into propagandists, into 'engineers of the human soul'.[3]

During the Weimar Republic in Germany the arts flourished in an atmosphere of unprecedented creative freedom which affected the entire cultural *milieu* of Central Europe. Expressionist artists who had had their feverish beginnings in the years before and during the War, when they faced public hostilities and found only few collectors ready to acquire their works. The Expressionists, deeply affected by the carnage of trench warfare at the western front renewed their activities during the 1920s and gained recognition. Many of them did not live in the capital but worked in smaller cities, like Dresden, Frankfurt, Darmstadt and Hannover, where local museums began to establish collections of their paintings and sculptures. It was in Berlin where progressive ideas and social models were tested. Artists, intellectuals and political outsiders operating in this city believed in modernity, in the power of technology to solve the economic and social problems of their time. They were enthusiastic about American-style capitalism and its architectural and technological manifestations, but like their Russian counterparts admired 'Americanism' from afar and set their hopes in utopian Socialism. Parties on the left and the right of the political spectrum promoted perspectives for an evolutionary society focussed on the *typus* of 'new man' living in harmony with nature while reshaping the city in 'his own image', a capable worker and organiser of human progress. The promotion of sport, healthy living and hygiene reformed social expectations, affected fashions, trends and style as well as new types of individual and communal living. In its early years the Bauhaus in Weimar – in Dessau from 1926 onwards – was imbued with this idealism. The school developed under the directorship of the architect Walter Gropius into one of the most influential centres of art and design education. The example of its teaching methods and practice projected the modernist impulse throughout Europe. Amongst those who taught at the Bauhaus were abstract painters and designers dedicated to radical experimentation like Paul Klee, Vassili Kandinsky, Oskar Schlemmer and László Moholy-Nagy. Re-interpreting craft traditions, Bauhaus artists and students created prototypes in the field of applied art, industrial design and architecture, which were committed to the functionalist ethos.

Hitler's rise to power in 1933 unleashed a vengeful persecution of the avant-garde driven by a virulent anti-modernism. The cultural policies of the Nazi regime represented a petit-bourgeois backlash motivated by anti-left and anti-Semitic tendencies, with the aim to re-establish 'traditional' nineteenth century values. The art favoured by Hitler marked a return to the academic pseudo-romantic genres of the past. Modern art was condemned under the banner of 'Kulturbolschewismus', cultural bolshevism.[4] Under the slogan 'Entartete Kunst', Degenerate Art, a campaign was started against the art of the Weimar years, to uproot modernism and to undermine and destroy its cultural impact. It was orchestrated nationwide but was not only aimed at German art but at European modernism at large. Thousands of artworks were confiscated during the 1937 purges of museums and private galleries. Most of the works were auctioned off in Switzerland from where many of them found their way into American collections. Drawings and prints, considered particularly 'worthless', were burnt in 1939 by order of the Ministry of Propaganda in the courtyard of the Berlin Fire Brigade.

2.

The Second World War unleashed by Hitler and his cohorts threw Europe into a murderous abyss. The fall of Paris in 1940 marked not only the military defeat of France but symbolised also the end of the cultural hegemony of Europe. The exodus of artists and intellectuals, many of them Jews, that had begun in Germany in 1933, continued throughout Nazi occupied Europe. The most important destination of these refugees was the USA; artists, architects and scientists settled predominantly in New York City and Chicago, some of them joined the great Universities of Yale, Harvard and Berkeley.

Throughout the 1930s American society struggled to overcome the effects of the World Economic Crisis by implementing the social programmes of the 'New Deal' proposed by President F.D. Roosevelt. The Work Projects Administration, WPA, initiated large scale building and engineering projects to ease widespread unemployment. The Federal Art Project, a subdivision of the WPA which operated from 1935 to 1943, was established to help artists in need, by commissioning collaborative art projects like murals and public sculptures. Despite the existence, since 1928, of the Museum of Modern Art and the exemplary exhibition programmes devised by its director Alfred Barr, the WPA art projects remained virtually unaffected by modernism. The resulting works were mostly executed in a narrative realism, at times not dissimilar to Socialist Realism, or a kind of decorative figuration derived from the *Ecole de Paris*. The WPA system promoted American values and was therefore closed to European refugee artists; their modernist backgrounds and progressive tendencies did not fit the prevailing tastes and tendencies.

It fell to the architectural profession to implant international modernism into the USA. In the eyes of European architects and designers America's industrialised building systems, which had enabled the bold construction of steel framed skyscrapers, represented the ideal expression of Americanism. In turn, modernist concepts, the functionalist outlook and organisational skill of European architects found the admiration of their American counterparts. Arriving in the USA via Britain, László Moholy-Nagy settled in Chicago where he founded in 1937 the 'New Bauhaus',

later renamed 'Institute of Design'. Its very name was a declaration of his intention to make it the first school for art and design in America structured on the didactic principles and modernist ethics of its German predecessor. Chicago also welcomed Mies van der Rohe who opened his architectural practice in the city and became the driving forces behind the establishment of the 'Chicago School of Architecture'. Walter Gropius and Marcel Breuer established the 'Harvard Graduate School of Design'. It was no accident that German modernists were given the means to set up these schools. Gropius, Mies and Moholy, highly experienced designers and communicators, were able to attract onto their staff other members of Europe's artistic élite. Within a few years young Americans were reaping the benefit.

Not unlike Picasso and Braque, collaborators and rivals while developing Cubism during the 1910s, the artists Jackson Pollock and Willem de Kooning were engaged in the mid 1940s in a creative dialogue and the competitive production of abstract paintings that eventually were to define a new genre: Abstract Expressionism. These paintings rejected the descriptive conventions of the art of the previous decade. After the hardships and restrictions of the war years Abstract Expressionism, based on painterly actions and gestures, on the materiality of paint itself and pure colour values, signalled a new freedom in art. Painting came to represent the direct transfer and transformation of emotional energies onto canvas; be it, in the case of de Kooning, in the form of stabs and linear discharges or, in the case of Pollock, in the form of linear drips and calligraphic traces. Pollock said about his newly found existential position: 'Painting is a state of being… Painting is self-discovery. Every good painter paints what he is.'[5] Painters like Franz Kline, Lee Krasner, Joan Mitchell, Robert Motherwell, Mark Rothko, Barnett Newman,

Clyfford Still and others found their own ways into Abstract Expressionism. Their evolutionary leap was related to an altered awareness of drawing as action; the understanding of drawing as a spontaneous act that 'can make visible things that cannot be seen – states of mind, ideas, and processes.'[6]

Throughout the 1940s and 50s, as the cities of Germany, Italy and France were cleared of their war ruins and rebuilding began, modernism returned from America in a rejuvenated and advanced form. American Jazz and Abstract Expressionism arrived in post-war Europe in tandem with the Marshall Plan. American art was perceived as revolutionary, as a declaration of freedom. American artists participated in the first post-war Venice Biennale and exhibitions circulated by the Museum of Modern Art in the 1950s promoted the works of the New York School. European artists adopted Abstract Expressionism and transformed and re-interpreted its underlying concepts into 'Action Painting', 'Tachisme' and 'L'art informel'. American artists Mark Tobey and Cy Twombly, who came to work in Europe, established friendships with like-minded artists like Henri Michaux, Hans Hartung and Lucio Fontana.

During these formative years the transatlantic exchange of ideas and impulses between American and European artists was firmly established, which remained a dynamic cultural interaction that lasted throughout the second half of the twentieth century. The dialogue continues up to our days .

footnotes

1   Richard Huelsenbeck, *Dadaist Manifesto 1918*, in Robert Motherwell (ed.), *Dada Painters and Poets*, New York, 1951 p. 12.

2   Leaflet published by Direzione del Movimento Futurismo, Milan 11. March 1915.

3   'Comrade Stalin has described our writers as engineers of the human soul… Our task is to ideologically transform and re-educate working people in the spirit of Socialism. This method… we call Socialist Realism'. Andrei Shdanov in H.J.Schmitt and G.Schramm,(eds.), *Realismuskonzeptionen: Dokumente zum 1.Allunionskongress der Sowjetschriftsteller*, Frankfurt a. M., 1974.

4   'National Socialism has made it its primary task to rid the German people of all those influences which are fatal and ruinous to its existence…From now on we will wage an unrelenting war of purification against the last elements of putrefaction in our culture…' 'Der Führer eröffnet die Grosse Deutsche Kunstausstellung 1937', in *Die Deutsche Kunst im Dritten Reich*, vol.1, Munich 1937.

5   Bernice Rose, *Jackson Pollock, Drawing into Painting*, The Museum of Modern Art, New York 1980, p. 21.

6   Jack Flam, 'The Modern Drawing', in *New York Collects: Drawing and Watercolours, 1900-1950*. New York 1999, p.21.

13. Carlo Carra (1881-1966), *Boxer*, 1913

88. Emilio Vedova (1919-2006), 'No,No,No', 1969

44

44. Willem de Kooning (1904-1997), **Untitled**, 1966/67
© The Willem de Kooning Foundation, New York/ ARS, NY and DACS, London 2010

21. Dan Flavin (1933-1996), Sailboat, 1986

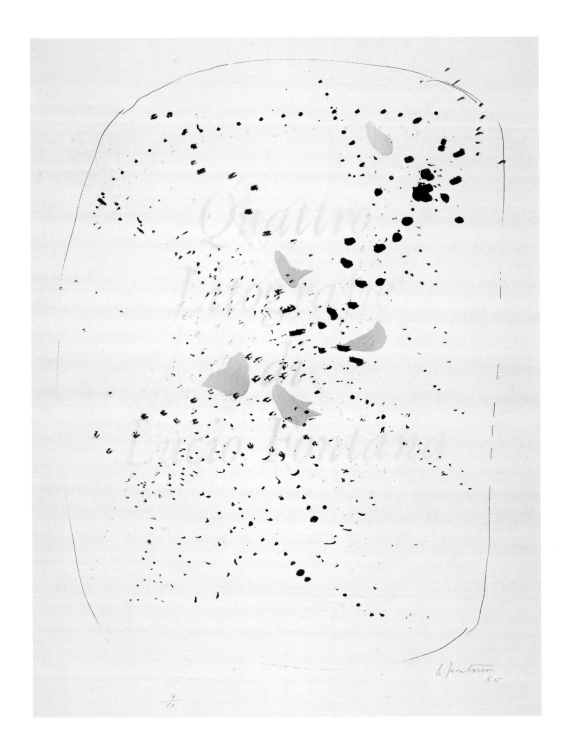

22. Lucio Fontana (1899-1968), **Plate one from 'Quattro Litografie'**, 1955
© Lucio Fontana/SIAE/DACS, London 2010

67. Jackson Pollock (1912-1956), **Untitled**, 1951
© The Pollock-Krasner Foundation ARS, NY and DACS, London 2009

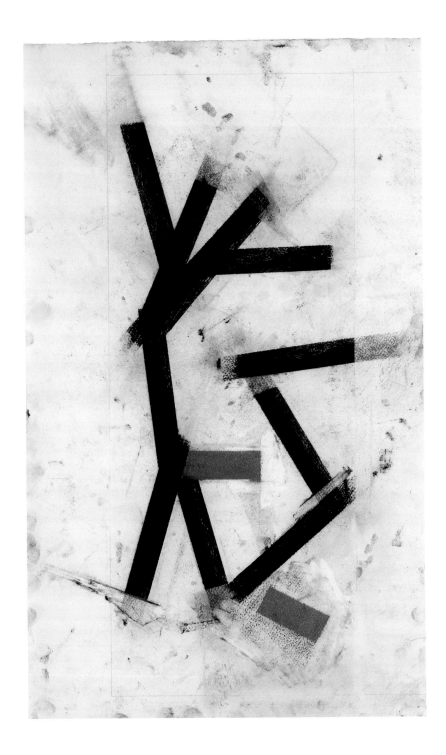

77. Joel Shapiro (b.1941), **Untitled**, 1994
© ARS, NY and DACS, London 2009

40. Franz Kline (1910-1962), Untitled, 1957/58
© ARS, NY and DACS, London 2010

50

56. Henri Michaux (1899-1984), **Composition** c1960-62 © ADAGP, Paris and DACS, London 2010

18. Jean Fautrier (1898-1964), **Sunset**, 1964 © ADAGP, Paris and DACS, London 2010

38. Linda Karshan (b.1947), **Untitled,** 25.06.1998

78. Kurt Sonderborg (1923-2008), **Untitled**, 1962

57. Joan Mitchell (1926-1992), **Untitled**, 1959/60

85. Cy Twombly (b. 1928), Untitled, 1971

2. William Anastasi (b.1933), **Subway Drawing**, 1967

83. Mark Tobey (1890-1976), **Night Celebration III**, 1971
© Estate of Mark Tobey, ARS, NY/DACS, London, 2010

1. Maliheh Afnan (b.1935), **Blackboard**, 1987

31. Philip Guston (1913-1980), **Hooded**, 1968

From 'Modern' to 'Contemporary'

David Elliott

How much do the words we use to describe art affect our ways of looking at it and do these words remain the same, regardless of the time in which we live? Art is formed by, reflects and gives an image of the time in which it is made but, if it is any good, it will also transcend its time and will be valued, perhaps for completely different reasons, in the future. Words, too, can be ambiguous and may have a number of different meanings, some of which are inconsistent. How do we reflect this in the frameworks we create to look at, think about and exhibit art?

For many people the idea of 'modern' art is consigned to the past in that they feel that it reflects a western belief in progress that has since been superseded by the more flexible and pluralistic categories of 'post-modern' and 'contemporary'. Speed of communication has shrunk the way we look at the world, but at the same time, to some, it also seems a larger, more unsettling place because the west no longer quite dominates it in the same way. The same is true about art. 'Modern art' is not as closed a category as its detractors claim and it may be that 'post-modern' and 'contemporary' art are as much a continuation of as a rupture from their previous intellectual and cultural heritage. But the world is changing rapidly and with it our idea of what constitutes contemporary reality. Without doubt this is having an impact on how we look at art.

The history of modernity has been written as a linear narrative privileging the inevitability of the present. In this story of remorseless progress one development succeeded the next. But the discontinuous, chaotic and polyvalent activity of making art has never supported this view. The dissolution of the idea of progress is perhaps one of the most important contributions of post-modernism. What has been put in its place is an idea of history and culture as a field or matrix in which many different links can be made across time and space.

Now when the Digital Revolution is having as large and far-reaching an impact as the Industrial Revolution in the eighteenth century, when 'diversity', 'pluralism', the 'multicultural' and the 'global' are overused cultural mantras – in a 'post-modern', 'post-soviet', 'post-colonial' world – we struggle to find the right words and concepts to describe the ways in which our culture has changed. To complicate the matter further, the idea of the 'post-modern' with its reference to previous hierarchies and systems of power has been replaced by the more open and flexible category of the 'contemporary' that can be used to refer to all art made in the present and relatively recent past. There is no consensus about when contemporary art begins, or even what it is. It may refer to the present or very recent past; in other cases, particularly with regard to collections of museums of contemporary art, it may go back as far as the end of the Second World War or the beginning of the 1960s. But the scope of the term 'contemporary' very much depends on the location of the institution. Museums of Contemporary Art in Cambridge and Canton (Guangzhou) would tell two very different stories.

It is clear, though, at a time when art, its history and reception are in a state of flux, the institutions that preserve, collect and present art need, in their turn, to be both dynamic and reactive. This has had an impact on the many different kinds of modern art museums built across the world. Some aspire to be like temples for the converted – aloof from the crowd, others adopt the character of treasure houses, intent on protecting and displaying their precious hoards, still others are more like malls where the visitor can 'consume' art, some are prescriptively didactic, others are ashamedly partisan and yet others seem to be much more valued for their shell, their architecture, than what they actually do or contain. But, if they are not to become museum pieces in themselves, they have to be able to adapt the frameworks through which they view and display art to reflect its changed perspectives, circumstances and meanings.

It was not always like this. The first public collections of modern art compiled at the beginning of the twentieth century in the State Museums in Berlin by Hugo von Tschudi and the towns of Hagen and then Essen by the collector Karl Ernst Osthaus were made by partisan, driven and uncompromising people who never questioned the rightness of their taste in the face of censorship or official disapproval. At the end of the 1920s, against the background of a world economic slump, the Founder Trustees of the Museum of Modern Art in New York appointed the twenty-seven year old Alfred H. Barr Jr. as its first director. Here, away from the conflicts of Europe, life and art seemed simpler, objectives more clear. After 1929 MoMA quickly created frameworks or categories for displaying and thinking about art that many others subsequently sought to emulate. Following the totalising model of the German Bauhaus, an art school that taught and made links between all of the visual arts, Barr set up a multi-departmental museum that covered film, photography,

architecture and design as well as painting, sculpture and works on paper. His aim was to research, exhibit, collect and promote the most advanced and 'best' art being made at the time. Barr and his staff were essentially connoisseurs of objects made within a new field of which sense had to be made by creating some kind of relative hierarchy or order. The educational and constructive role of the museum was stressed from the outset.

Modernity then was not the problematic or historical concept it is regarded as today. But its meaning was still slippery and from the outset Barr was quick to realise that as a term it was both 'ambiguous and flexible'. There has never been complete agreement about when was 'modern', but in relation to culture it has increasingly been applied to European and world history since the eighteenth century Enlightenment. This was a time of intellectual, political, social and cultural ferment which witnessed the end of the dominance of monarchy by divine right to be replaced by elective democracy based on ideas of individual responsibility, autonomy and freedom, mirrored to a greater or lesser extent by the rise of the sovereign nation state. This was set against the background of the social and economic effects of the Industrial Revolution, a dramatic rise in population and the appropriation for profit and power of undeveloped lands. Underwriting all of this was a firm belief in (western) civilization and progress, supported by discoveries in science and technology and the power of rational thought.

Although very much a child of the modern tradition, Barr did not feel inclined to extend the new macro-category of modern art as far back as the eighteenth century because until the middle of nineteenth century the art had already been accepted by collectors, museums and the public alike. He was far more interested in the kind of hyper-modern art

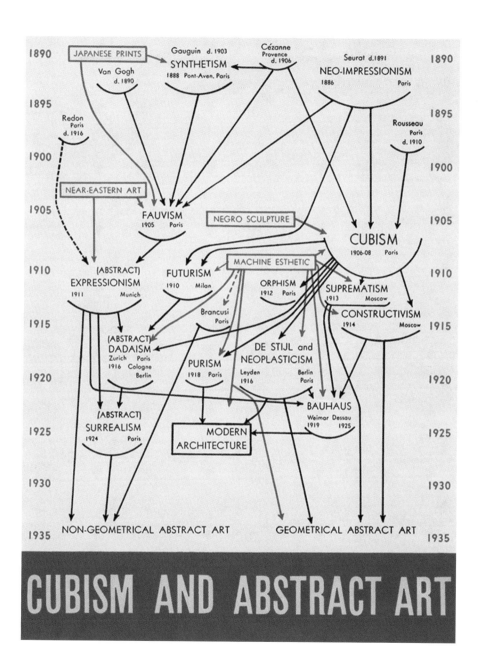

Alfred. H. Barr Jr., a Chart of Modern Art
catalogue cover for his exhibition Cubism and Abstract Art, Museum of Modern Art, New York, 1936

that had emerged in the avant-garde that had not yet been absorbed into American culture.

The birth of the avant-garde, a term taken over first from the military and then from radical politics, both anticipated and ran parallel to vast changes in cultural consciousness throughout the nineteenth century and became one of the main engines for regeneration in modernity. Combining vital elements of continuity, in that it was self-renewing, and change, in that it acted as both a focus and generator for 'discoveries' of new and radical approaches, each one superseding the other, it drove culture forward. In art history these different manifestations of hyper-modernity, combined with rational ideas about planning and society, subsequently came to be categorised as 'Modernism' – a kind of collective academy of the avant-garde. But, the words 'modern' and 'modernist' have often been confused and at times have even been understood to mean the same thing.

By the 1880s ideas about realism in modern art had moved away from the historic or literal desire to show the world as it was or should be, towards an oppositional and aesthetic concern with individual feeling and consciousness on the one hand and with a collective interest in structure or relationship on the other. For artists, as also with scientists and philosophers, the realisation had dawned that reality lay below the surface and had more to do with relativity – the relationship of one element to another, consciousness – different, competing modes of thought or perception, and sensibility – emotion, compulsion or conviction.

Barr captured the art of his own times and then tried to fit it into the past yet, inevitably, his perspectives were challenged by both more conservative and more radical artists and critics. Famously, he characterised his new museum as a

kind of artwork in itself: a torpedo forging ahead, cutting through time and space. Two seminal exhibitions *Cubism and Abstract Art* (1936) and *Fantastic Art, Dada and Surrealism* (1936-7) laid out his understanding of the development of modern art to that time. On the dust jacket of the former catalogue, a *Chart of Modern Art* set down such artists as Seurat, Gauguin, Cézanne and Van Gogh as the forerunners of the opposing tendencies of Fauvism and Cubism that could then be traced down, through many other styles, to the emergence of geometrical and non-geometrical abstract art. Abstraction in one form or another seemed to be an inevitable end of modern art.

In this approach Barr was adapting traditional stylistic and chronological analytical methods of art history while consigning the subject of the work to a secondary position. In this the British critics Roger Fry and Clive Bell, who laid great stress on the significance of form, had influenced him. Yet he was also very much aware of art's political meanings and affiliations.

Abstraction can no longer be regarded as an end in itself but purely as a means used by some artists to move from a world of perception to one of pictorial space with its own rules and logic. Non-objectivity, too, moves away from perception towards rational concepts of underlying geometry, structures, even engineering, industrial, social and metaphorical. And realism itself is hardly ever 'real' but a means of approaching ideas, phenomena and relationships that we can all recognise but from differing viewpoints. Such categories no longer have any pretension to be definitive, universal or even consistent – good art can never be confined – only to provide a complex and accessible way of looking at the development of modern and contemporary art by relating it to basic ideas that we all understand. Devoid of previous cast iron certainties, it may seem that contemporary art has become increasingly alienated from modern art; but do they really belong to such different worlds when to a great extent, in its polyvalence and diversity, modern art anticipated contemporary culture and consciousness?

Barr's programme at the Museum of Modern Art during the 1930s reflected a wide global interest but the changed climate of the Second World War and post-war years and the rise of the New York School subsequently led to a greater concentration on the progression of American and European Modernism. This only began to crumble during the mid-1970s when the idea of either a progressive political or artistic avant-garde no longer seemed to hold water. What did slowly become clear was that in its views of the world, as well as in its standards of living, the West was the heir to the benefits and curses of the European Enlightenment. Capitalism or Communism seemed to be little more than different faces of the same intellectual coin, each extreme needing the other for its own self definition, and each in practice behaving equally badly.

Those who lived on the Atlantic Rim had been 'masters of the universe', many of whom had single-mindedly pursued their interests with arrogance, cruelty and greed. Yet one of the positive legacies of the Enlightenment had been the creation of a receptive and open matrix of ideas and beliefs within which modern and contemporary art could flourish. The idea of autonomy, independence and freedom for both art and artist grew out of the same intellectual and political ferment that fuelled the movement for Human Rights. From the at times ambiguous, complicated and confounding concepts of autonomy and freedom, modern and contemporary art have derived their power – the disinterested power of a reflective and creative individual voice.

Recently, with the rapid economic growth of China and India and the slow dissolution of Enlightenment certainties about its entitlement and destiny, power has started to be more widely dispersed across the globe; a strong aesthetic impact is accordingly being felt. Unlike modern art, contemporary art will no longer be dominated by purely western models and values as we learn to appreciate the work of artists whose names we can barely pronounce. Long standing and established, the western tradition will hardly evaporate but, in a world shrunken by travel, internet and digital communication, it will have to share space with the contemporary art of equally established cultures that have differing priorities and views not only of the world, but also of how power should be used, and of the kinds of beauty enshrined within it.

Berlin, December, 2009.

86. Nadezhda Udaltsova (1886-1961), Composition, 1916

MODERNITY, ARCHITECTURE, AND THE CITY

Iain Boyd Whyte

> Ideology collapses and vanishes, utopianism atrophies,
> but something great is left behind: *the memory of a hope*.
> Henri Lefebvre

At first glance it may seem odd to include an essay on architectural modernism in the catalogue to an exhibition of drawings. The discourse on architecture, however, and its very tangible response to the challenges both of modernity and of modernism, might be regarded as an exemplary case, which throws its penetrating light across the broader landscape of cultural production in the twentieth century.

modernity

'Modern' has many meanings. It means current and actual, as opposed to former, previous, or foregoing. It means self-consciously new in contrast to old. More negatively, it is used to describe the passing, transient, and merely fashionable, in contrast to the eternal. With the insight that cultural production is transient comes the awareness that the modern age commenced at varying points for the different arts and sciences. Diderot, for example, in the article 'Moderne', in his *Encyclopédie ou dictionnaire raisonné des sciences, des art et des métiers* (1751-72), proposed that modern literature began with Boëthius in the fifth century, modern astronomy with Copernicus, modern philosophy with Descartes, and modern physics with Newton. It could be argued that modern architecture also began with Newton, or more exactly with the emergence in the later eighteenth century of rationalism as the dominant force in social, political, and scientific discourse.

If we are to believe the post-modernist account in general, and Jean-François Lyotard in particular, the Enlightenment project was a single, holistic conspiracy of uncontrolled reason, intent on the domination of man and nature through the workings of technology, against the ultimate good of mankind. Critics of this position, most notably Jürgen Habermas, have responded that the Enlightenment project of a world guided by reason was never a monolithic enterprise, but rapidly evolved into a separatist culture, with experts responsible for specific intellectual spheres, and fundamental divisions emerging between the three main forms of human thinking: science, morality, and art – forms that before the Enlightenment had been rolled together into a single world-view under the influence of religious or metaphysical principles.

Developing the more differentiated reading of Habermas, four themes might be identified as characteristic of modernity, which align themselves into two diametrically opposed groupings. Individualism and relativism on one hand – understood as the absence of any absolute values – are challenged by the authoritarian demands of instrumental reason and capitalism on the other – the demands of technological progress, cost-efficiency, and a docile labour market. Each of these four conditions are essentially modernist, yet in a state of total opposition to its inimical pair. Precisely this conflict led Karl Marx to the celebrated observation, made in 1856: 'On the one hand there have started into life industrial and scientific forces which no epoch of human history has ever suspected. On the other hand, there exist symptoms of decay, surpassing the horrors of the latter times of the Roman Empire. In our days everything is pregnant with its contrary.'[1] According to the Marxist account, the dialectical and confrontational nature of modernity simply reflected the demands of the ruling class, which had a vested interest not only in change, but in crisis and chaos, characterised by Marx himself as 'uninterrupted disturbance, everlasting uncertainty and agitation'. Stability or stasis in the world of the capitalist entrepreneur means slow death. Modernity is thus marked by the unprecedented pace and scope of change and the emergence of new and unprecedented social institutions structured around the imperatives of the post-feudal society.

modernism

The creative response to modernity is modernism. Given the contested nature of modernity, it is unsurprising to find that modernism operates under similar conditions of ambiguity and irresolution. In the specific context of architecture, any account of modernism must be grounded on a careful analysis of the emotional and intellectual parameters within which the architects are working. The explicator of architectural modernism must consider the relationship of architecture and of architects to three key epistemological positions: history, theology, and politics.

history

In their understanding of history, both the conservative anti-modernist and the radical modernist share closely similar convictions, albeit with opposing motives. For the architect working in the nineteenth and twentieth centuries, history was understood not as a sequence of discrete events but as an agency with its own, irrefutable patterns, laws, and logic. Replacing the Christian belief in progressive revelation, architecture turned to Neo-Hegelian historicism to explain the significance of the particular building or constructional technique within broader laws of progress. This process is well expressed in Mandelbaum's definition of historicism as 'the belief that an adequate understanding of the nature of any phenomenon and an adequate assessment of its value are to be gained by considering it in terms of the place which it occupied and the role which it played within a process of development.'[2] Following the imperatives of historicism, architecture was understood as a significant expression of the Hegelian 'world spirit', the essence of which is movement, and thus history. The built fabric, accordingly, was seen as an expression of the life of previously held positions in the unfolding of history. The Hegelian position refutes relativism or the idea that one view is simply equivalent or relative to another, since all ideas are interconnected in the unfolding of the history of human culture and society. Even views that are sharply hostile to one another constitute, to the Hegelian, merely opposite determinations of the same spirit, the positive and negative of the same proposition. And these determinations, in turn, are the inevitable expressions of the *Zeitgeist*, the spirit of the age, expressing the concept of the sense or rationality in the order of things and the succession of one state of affairs after another according to some kind of lawful process.[3]

With architecture understood as a component in the Hegelian history of the spirit – architects became fired in the nineteenth century by a strong belief in the particularity of the present moment and by the conviction that the revolutionary moment is imminent. For the conservative, this is a moment of terror, when the values and traditions built up over the centuries and millennia will be brought tumbling down by the forces of revolution, understood primarily as destruction. For the radical, the revolutionary moment promises change, the redefinition of goals, and the banishment of historical prejudices and injustices. By the end of the twentieth century, this all-dominating explicatory *Zeitgeist* fell from favour. As an expression of the *grand récit* of historical progress, it was rejected by the post-modern critique. At more or less the same time, it was also attacked by conservative architectural historiography. David Watkin, for example, in *Morality and Architecture*, first published in 1977, saw it as evidence of a Germanic and Pevsnerian conspiracy: 'The underlying principle remains the same throughout Pevsner's work: art must "fit" into the *Zeitgeist* which is now a progressivist harbinger of the earthly new Jerusalem.'[4]

Far from being the invention of the historians, however, the architects themselves, particularly in the gestatory decades of architectural modernism, were firmly attached to the Hegelian and historicist account. Otto Wagner, for example, giving his inaugural lecture to the Academy of Fine Arts in Vienna in 1894 insisted that: 'The starting point of every artistic creation must be the needs, ability, and achievements of our time.'[5] A few years later in 1898, his pupil Joseph Olbrich designed the Secession building in Vienna, which carried above the door the inscription: *'Der Zeit ihre Kunst: Der Kunst ihre Freiheit'* – To the Age its Art: To Art its Freedom. Similar sentiments are legion among the threorists of early modernism, stressing the inseparable bond between architecture and the *Zeitgeist*. In this relationship, the architect functioned as a seismograph, highly and predictively responsive to the demands and the spirit of the age. Launching *L'Esprit Nouveau* in October 1920, Le Corbusier, very predictably, hailed the particularity of the moment: 'There is a new spirit: it is the spirit of construction and of synthesis, guided by a clear conception. Whatever may be thought of it, it animates to-day the great part of human society.'[6] In the Soviet Union,

too, the search for the style to match the spirit of the age was equally strong, and informs the very title of Moisei Ginzburg's seminal book, *Style and Epoch*, which drew strongly on the Wöfflinian thesis that style in the visual arts and architecture was the direct expression of the spirit of a time and of a people.[7]

This essentially Hegelian position dominated the architectural mindset for the great majority of the twentieth century. When the British group Archigram were proselytising in the late 1960s for an architecture that was lightweight, technically sophisticated, and highly mobile, they were responding, self-confessedly, to the spirit of the age, encapsulated at the time by the moon-shot on one hand, and 1960s pop-culture on the other. It is hard to imagine how it might have been otherwise, as the imperatives of modernity demand of the creative spirit a direct engagement with the technological inventions of the age. To bemoan an indifference to historical models, as both conservative and post-modernist theoreticians did in the final decades of the century, denies these imperatives and wilfully misunderstands the nature of the modernist project. The inevitable result was the feeble, formalist posturings of post-modern architecture, devoid of any theoretical basis within the discipline itself, beyond a misinformed condemnation of modernism.

theology

Paradise on earth was the explicit goal of the early architectural modernism. Writing in 1902, the cultural sociologist Georg Simmel noted among his contemporaries a specific 'yearning after a final object' in a context that 'no longer renders possible its attainment.' And this, he says, produces 'specifically modern feelings, that life has no meaning, that we are driven hither and thither in a mechanism built up out of mere preliminary stages and means, that the final and absolute wherein consists the reward of living, ever escapes our grasp.'[8] Both the brave new world of technology and the return to the wooden-framed cottage represent a search for certainty in a modern world that is categorically unable to provide such reassurance.

This search for certainty and, indeed, for some form of spiritual reassurance is central to the dynamics of modernism in general and modernist architecture in particular. Following the triumph of Enlightenment science in the eighteenth century and the decline of organised religion in the later nineteenth century when faced with the Darwinist challenge, the grand spiritual narratives were left in dysfunctional tatters. In the resulting vacuum countless specialist interests joined the fray, ranging from teetotalism and vegetarianism to dance and neo-Buddhism, each offering itself as the holistic response. The problems of the world would be solved if only the people would learn to dance or to shun the temptations of meat or alcohol. Architecture was another of these partial systems, proposing itself as a total solution. Spiritual certainty and social harmony were to be achieved by good design, and the architect would take on a messianic role as the divinely gifted individual empowered to redirect and reconstruct the goals and ambitions of the industrial society. As Le Corbusier insisted in the *Charter of Athens*: 'Architecture holds the key to everything.'

In its spiritual ambitions, modernist architecture fed on deeply-ingrained, Judeo-Christian ideas of progress, which understood history as a single, future-directed progression that would find its fulfilment in 'final' events such as the coming of the Messiah or the Last Judgement. As Karl Löwith has argued, the central modern idea of progress is simply a secularised version of ideas that derived from medieval Christianity: 'The ideal of modern science of mastering the forces of nature and the idea of progress emerged neither in the classical world nor in the East, but

in the West. But what enabled us to remake the world in the image of man? Is it perhaps that the belief in being created in the image of a Creator-God, the hope in a future kingdom of God, and the Christian command to spread the gospel to all nations for the sake of salvation have turned into a secular presumption that we have to transform the world into a better world?'[9] This presumption is central to the mindset of architectural modernism, with its lingering belief in messianic leadership, its insistent emphasis on progress and expectation, and its biblical patterns of guilt and expectation.

politics

A centrist, reformist socialism was the dominant political voice of the early decades of architectural modernism. As Bruno Taut sensed in 1919: 'A feeling exists, or at least slumbers in all of us, …that one should feel a sense of solidarity with all men. Socialism in the non-political, supra-political sense is the simple, straightforward relationship between men, far removed from any form of domination. It straddles the divide between warring classes and nations and binds all men together.'[10] In a similar tone Le Corbusier concluded *Vers une architecture* in 1923 with the binary choice between good, which is to say Modernist, Corbusian design, or political revolution. In accord with its revisionist socialist roots, the white modernism of the 1920s has traditionally been equated politically with social democracy and the liberal left. The great housing estates of Berlin and Frankfurt, for example, built under the aegis of the respective chief city architects, Martin Wagner and Ernst May, forged a concrete link between progressive architectural practice and the socialism of both city government and trade unionism. In contrast, the architecture of the dictatorships, as it evolved in the 1930s in the Soviet Union, Germany, and Italy, was seen to forge an inseparable link between monumental Neo-Classicism, stylistic conservatism, and totalitarianism. This was the simple, good/bad scenario argued right up into the 1960s and 1970s, and paraphrased in Pevsner's celebrated admonition that any word devoted to Nazi architecture is a word too many. Only when the modernist project in architecture began to crumble in the 1960s under the weight of its own dullness, did the historiography begin to question the simple, moralistic account of good modernism and bad Neo-Classicism. This questioning operated at many levels, from the simple biographic through to more sophisticated theoretical enquiries. Biographically, such issues as Le Corbusier's relationship with the pro-Nazi Vichy government in France, or the initial willingness of the German avant-garde to enter Nazi-run design competitions became the subject of scholarly enquiry.

At the instrumental level, scholars like Boris Groys investigated the relationship between the avant-garde and the dictators not as one of opposites, but of similarity: 'totalitarian art was so unyielding towards the avant-garde, because it itself was inspired by an avant-garde purpose.'[11] The mutual purpose was a planned world, infatuated with technology and responsive to the dictates of an élite that promised a new world and a new social order, invented either on the architect's drawing board or in the corridors of political power. At an even more general level, revisionist sociologists like Zygmunt Bauman proposed that the entire Enlightment project, far from being an emancipatory force for mankind, was a single, 'holistic' conspiracy of uncontrolled reason, working ultimately against the good of mankind.

In this light, the architecture of high modernism takes on a more sinister character. Were the broad avenues, regular blocks, and broad expanses of glass favoured by the 1920s avant-garde dedicated to the emancipation of mankind in a new world of light, air, and transparency, or was architecture being corrupted into yet another agency of surveillance and control? At the level of intentionality, were the iconoclastic rebuilding plans of the modernists – Le Corbusier's *Voisin* plan for Paris, or Ludwig Hilberseimer's scheme for central Berlin – which demanded the destruction of large areas of the old city, essential preconditions and precursors for the dictatorial re-planning of Moscow, Berlin, and Rome in the 1930s?

Revisionist questions work on both sides of the equation. If architectural modernism was not as far removed from totalitarianism as its early histories suggested, then might monumental Neo-Classicism have a more complicated status than allowed it as the architectural expression of dictatorship? In their famous 1932 exhibition at the Museum of Modern Art in New York, Henry-Russell Hitchcock and Philip Johnson, defined and illustrated the 'International Style' with the work of architects like Le Corbusier, Walter Gropius, Mies van der Rohe, Erich Mendelsohn, and J.J.P. Oud. In terms, however, of its geographical distribution and the sheer volume of buildings, it would be equally possible to see the pared-down Neo-Classical revival as the international style of the 1930s.

The historian of modernist architecture not only has to acknowledge the dictatorial elements of high modernism in the 1920s and the universality of the Neo-Classical revival in the 1930s, but also the ambiguities endemic to the cultural and social policies of the dictatorships. These ambiguities are the inevitable result of the contradictions that lay at the heart of the totalitarian regimes: the desire to be both familiar and autocratic, to be technocratic yet wedded to the values of the soil, to be centralist yet alert to regional difference, to be, in short, all things to all people. Expressed in works of architecture, these contradictions allow the ultra-modernist *Rationalismo* of Terragni to coexist with the Imperial Roman pastiche of Mussolini's Italy, or modernist factories, folksy Hitler Youth hostels, and Neo-Romanesque autobahn bridges to be hailed as equivalent expressions of the spirit of National Socialism.

the city

As contradiction is fundamental to both modernity and modernism, it is hard to avoid the conclusion that the terms themselves are of relatively little use in establishing parameters or definitions. The power and fascination of modernity lie precisely in this dynamic irresolution, and modernism can only be investigated within the shifting parameters of modernity. Yet it is ultimately fruitless to indulge the possibility of limitless readings of modernity and modernism, and the historian or theorist of twentieth century architecture needs to construct contexts or matrices within which the antimonies of both modernity and of modernist architecture can be located and studied. The most fruitful context of enquiry to date has been the city. As James Donald has noted: 'Modernity is inherently both rational and mythical. Nowhere is this more evident than in the modern city.'[12] The dialectic thus established is between rationality and enchantment, the city of the planner and engineer against the city of the artist, the poet, and the flâneur. This is the conflict identified by Max Weber in *The Protestant Ethic and the Spirit of Capitalism*, who condemned the planned city driven by formal, means/end rationality as an 'iron cage' for the human spirit, from which all the magic has been driven out in a process of *Entzauberung* – disenchantment.

Weber's position was grounded in a long tradition of negative critiques of the industrial city, which flourished most vigorously in nineteenth-century Britain, the first heavily-industrialised society. Ruskin, bemoaned in 'The Nature of Gothic' that: 'The great cry that rises from all our manufacturing cities, louder than their furnace blast, is…that we manufacture everything there except men; we blanch cotton, strengthen steel, and refine sugar, and shape pottery; but to brighten, to strengthen, to refine, or to form a single living spirit, never enters into our estimate of advantages.'[13] Responding to this challenge, Ebenezer Howard's New Town impulse in the early years of the new century sought to combine the social advantages of the city with the primal innocence of the country: 'The town is the symbol of society – of mutual help and friendly co-operation…of broad, expanding sympathies, of science, art, culture, religion. And the country! … All that we are and all that we have comes from it. … It is the source of all health, all wealth, all knowledge. But its fullness of joy and wisdom has not yet revealed itself to man.'[14] Similar arguments resurfaced after World War I, with the reactionary modernists in Weimar Germany, where the likes of Heinrich Tessenow, Paul Schmitthenner, and Paul Schultze-Naumburg fell under the spell of the cultural pessimism typified by Oswald Spengler's *Decline of the West*. Alvar Aalto and the Scandinavian modernists would also play a significant part in this anti-urbanist geneaology in the 1930s; their influence resonated in the post-war New Town movement in Britain, with its dispersed site planning, brick housing, and homey 'people's detailing'.

The opposite reaction at the other extreme of the dialectic, responds positively and affirmatively to the industrial city and to the technological, demographic, and social forces that have created it. One of the earliest, and certainly the most celebrated affirmations of the metropolis as the defining site of modernity was that of Charles Baudelaire. In *Le peintre de la vie moderne*, first published in 1859, he offers the memorable sentence: 'By modernity I mean the ephemeral, the fugitive, the contingent, the half of art whose other half is the eternal and the immutable.'[15] For Baudelaire the new metropolis, Hausmann's Paris, was both exciting and heroic, and this heroism lay precisely in the transient qualities of modern life, in the world of fashion, the chance encounter on the Boulevard, the dazzling randomness of the great city. The nomadic sense of placelessness and flux that inevitably resulted from these qualities of transience were also reasons for celebration in the eyes of the rationalists. Otto Wagner, for example, presenting his extension to Vienna in 1911, praises anonymity as a particular quality of the metropolis. Such wholehearted commitment to the modernist city and to the technical and industrial forces that drive it, was shared by such names as Peter Behrens, Antonio Sant'Elia, Ludwig Hilberseimer, Martin Wagner, the high modernist Le Corbusier of the 1920s, the Soviet Constructivists, Adolf Meyer, Mart Stamm, Kenzo Tange, Cedric Price and the Archigram group of the late 1960s, and the prophets of High-Tech in the 1980s and 1990s: Norman Foster, Nicholas Grimshaw, Richard Rogers. Their message could be paraphrased in a passage from the 'Manifesto of Futurist Architecture', penned by Antonio Sant'Elia in 1914: 'Architecture now breaks with tradition. It must perforce make a new start. … We must invent and rebuild the Futurist city like an immense and tumultuous shipyard, agile, mobile, and dynamic in every detail; and the futurist house must be like a gigantic machine.'[16]

Moving from the simple, binary opposition of urbanites versus anti-urbanites, many sets of opposing poles offers itself: rationalists versus enchanters, engineers versus organicists, machine versus handcrafts, the straight boulevard versus the picturesquely serpentine street, flat roof versus pitched roof. These in turn combine with the political, theological, and historical positions previously touched on. Le Corbusier, in describing his visions of the city of the future in the 1920s, argued that the essence of his highly mechanistic grid-plan for the city was organic, in that it reflected the replication of cell-forms in nature. A recent commentator on Ludwig Mies van der Rohe has also argued most cogently that the Mies of the 1920s might be understood as an organicist, resistant to predetermined forms and open to organic processes of

becoming. According to this reading, Mies saw the city as 'a figure of totality and integration, symbol of the all-embracing but intangible structure, the unity of relationships and interdependences between things that he sought to express in material form and to make palpable for the beholder. Like many others of his generation, Mies invoked the figure of the organicism to refer precisely to such a holistic and unified relational structure. Based on the organic prinicple of free relation among self-determined parts, the model of the organicism could be applied to machines and machine-like cities as well as to plants.'[17] The contradictions pile up; the examples are endless.

conclusion

Modernism in architecture, as in all the arts, exists only as a response to the contradictory conditions of modernity. To understand the modernist statement, it is essential in every single case to go back to the condition of modernity that prompted the statement. Stripped of this relationship, modernism becomes an empty formalism, just another chrome-steel chair. Yet paradoxically, precisely the working out anew of formal relationships is the triumph of modernism, of an art that refuses to imitate the production and thus the conditions of any preceding generation. As Peter Bürger has noted: 'The category of artistic modernism *par excellence* is form. In modernism, form is not something pre-given which the artist must fulfil and whose fulfilment the critics and the educated public could check more or less closely against a canon of fixed rules. It is always an individual result, which the work represents.'[18] For the historian, the task of understanding and description must investigate the real-world context of the modernist production and re-establish, if only at the theoretical level, the fusion of art and life to which the twentieth-century avant-garde constantly aspired, and which it invariably failed to achieve. For the architect, the goal must be the affirmation of the essential categories of modernism, while freeing them from modernist rigidity and reinvesting them with life. Although penned in the context of literature, Malcolm Bradbury's conclusion is equally pertinent to architecture: 'Modernism is our art; it is the one art that responds to the scenario of our chaos.'[19]

footnotes

1   Karl Marx, Speech at the Anniversary of the People's Paper (1856), in: Robert C. Tucker (ed.), The Marx-Engels Reader, 2nd edition, New York, Norton, 1978, pp. 577-578.

2   Maurice Mandelbaum, History, Man, and Reason: A Study in Nineteenth-Century Thought, Baltimore, Johns Hopkins Press, 1971, p. 42.

3   Hegel understood this rationality as a spirit that animated people, not as a creation of human labour. See, Georg Wilhelm Friedrich Hegel, Elements of the Philosophy of Right, § 344, edited by Alan W. Wood, trans. H. B. Nisbet, Cambridge, Cambridge University Press, 1991, p. 373: The states, nations, and individuals involved in this business of the world spirit emerge with their own particular and determinate principles, which has its interpretation and actuality in their constitution and throughout the whole extent of their condition. In their consciousness of this actuality and in their preoccupation with its interests, they are at the same time the unconscious instruments and organs of that inner activity in which the shapes which they themselves assume pass away, while the spirit in and for itself prepares and works its way towards the transition to its next and higher stage.

4   David Watkin, Morality and Architecture, Oxford, Clarendon Press, 1977, p. 81.

5   Otto Wagner, Inaugural address to the Academy of Fine Arts, Vienna, 15 October 1894, quoted: Otto Wagner, Modern Architecture, trans. Harry Francis Mallgrave, Santa Monica, Getty Center Publications, 1988, p. 160.

6   Le Corbusier, Programme of L'Esprit Nouveau, no. 1 (October, 1920), quoted: Towards a New Architecture, trans. Frederick Etchells (1927), reprint: London, Architectural Press, 1946, p. 101.

7   For a discussion of the impact on Soviet Constructivism of German notions of the Zeitgeist derived from Riegl, Wölfflin, Frankl, and Spengler, see: Anatole Senkevitch, 'Introduction: Mosei Ginzburg and the Emergence of a Constructivist Theory of Architecture', in: Mosei Ginzburg, Style and Form, Cambridge, Mass., MIT Press, 1982, pp. 22-25.

8   Georg Simmel, 'Tendencies in German Life and Thought since 1870', International Monthly (New York), 5 (1902), p. 101; quoted: David Frisby, Fragments of Modernity, Cambridge, Polity, 1985, p. 43.

9   Karl Löwith, Meaning in History, Chicago, Chicago UP, 1949, p. 203.

10 Bruno Taut, Die Stadtkrone, Jena, Diederichs, 1919, pp. 59-60.

11 Boris Groys, 'Die totalitäre Kunst der 30er Jahre: Antiavantgardistisch in der Form und avantgardistisch im Inhalt', in: Jürgen Harten, Hans-Werner Schmidt, and Marie Luise Syring (eds.), exhibition catalogue, 'Die Axt hat geblüht …': Europäische Konflikte der 30er Jahre in Erinnerung an die frühe Avantgarde, Düsseldorf, Städtische Kunsthalle, 1987, p. 35.

12 James Macdonald, 'Metropolis: the City as Text', in: Robert Bocock and Kenneth Thompson (eds.), Social and Cultural Forms of Modernity, Cambridge, Polity, 1992, p. 437.

13 John Ruskin, 'The Nature of Gothic', in: The Stones of Venice, vol. 2., London, Dent, 1907, p. 151.

14 Ebenezer Howard, Garden Cities of To-Morrow (1898/1902) reprint, London, Faber & Faber, 1945, p. 48.

15 Charles Baudelaire, The Painter of Modern Life and Other Essays, trans. and ed. Jonathan Mayne, London, Phaidon, 1970, p. 13.

16 Antonio Sant'Elia, 'Manifesto of Futurist Architecture', in: Umbro Apollonio (ed.), Futurist Manifestos, London, Thames & Hudson, 1973, pp. 169, 170.

17 Detlef Mertins, 'Living in a Jungle: Mies, Organic Architecture, and the Art of City Building', in: Phyllis Lambert (ed.), Mies in America, New York, Abrams, 2002, p. 619.

18 Peter Bürger, The Decline of Modernism, University Park, Penn., Pennsylvania State University Press, 1992, p. 44.

19 Malcolm Bradbury and James McFarlane, 'The Name and Nature of Modernism', in: Bradbury and McFarlane (eds.), Modernism, Harmondsworth, Penguin, 1976, p. 27.

41. Gustav Klucis (1895-1938), **Architectural Study**, 1921/22

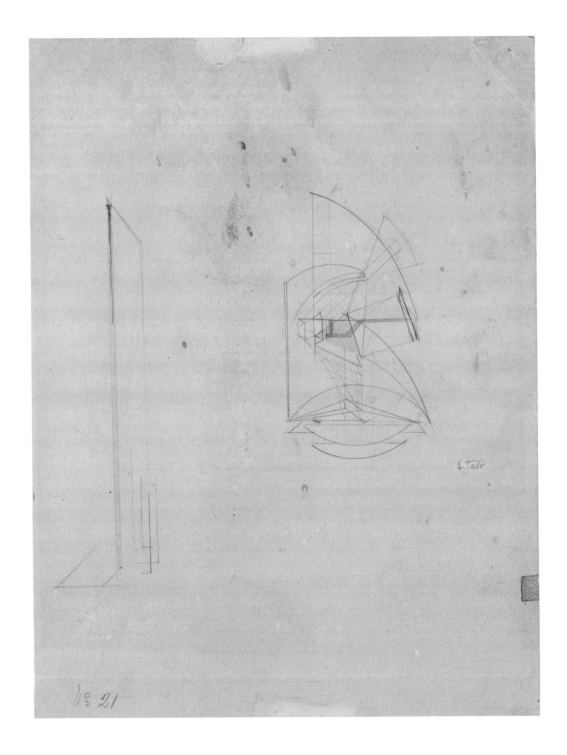

23. Naum Gabo (1890-1977), **Sketch for a Mobile Construction**, c1918
© Nina and Graham Williams, 2010

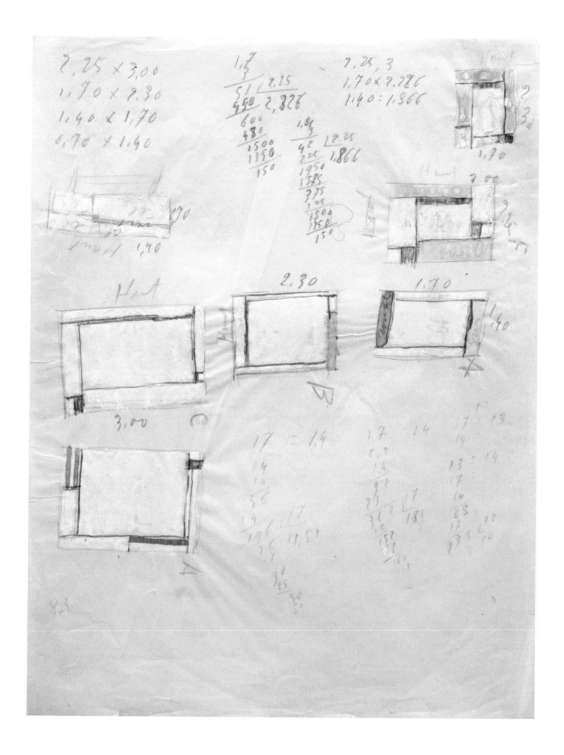

87. Georges Vantongerloo (1886-1965), Sketches, c.1936/37
© DACS, 2009

69. David Rabinowitch (b.1943), **Construction of Vision (2 colour properties, 2 tangents) VIII**, 1973
© ARS, NY and DACS, London 2010

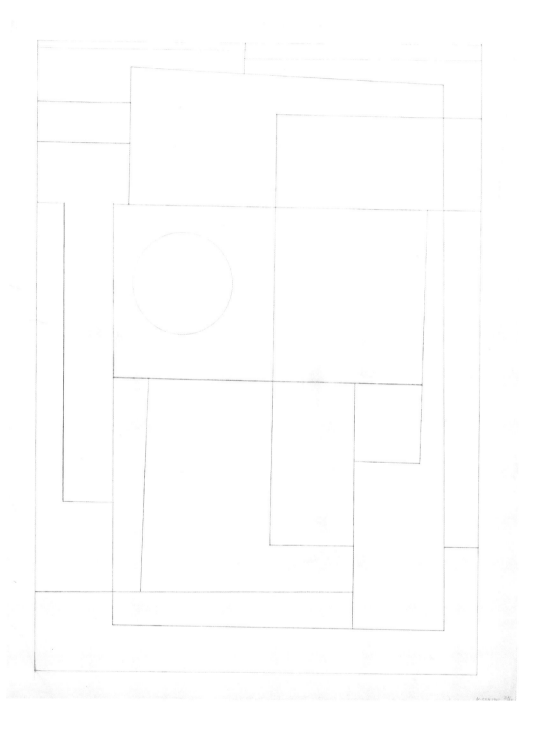

62. Ben Nicholson (1894-1982), **Drawing (Version 2)**, 1936
© Angela Verren Taunt, 2010

61. Ben Nicholson (1894-1982), **St. Rémy, Provence**, 1933 © Angela Verren Taunt, 2010

33. Barbara Hepworth (1903-1975), **St. Rémy, Provence**, 1933
© Bowness, The Estate of the Artist, 2010

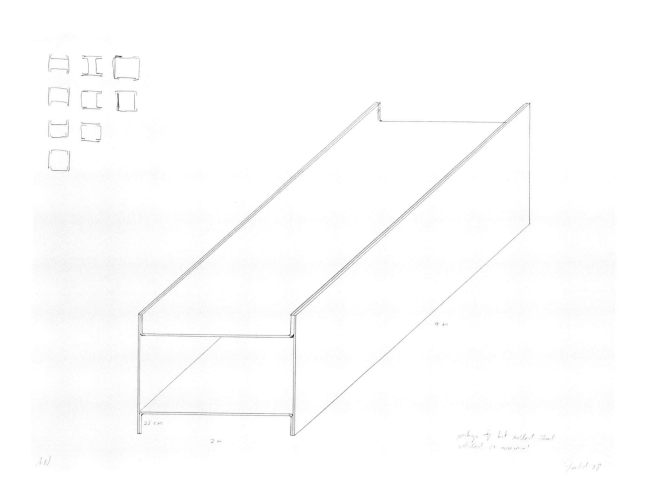

37. Donald Judd (1928-1994), Untitled, 1978
© Judd Foundation. Licensed by VAGA, New York/DACS, London 2009

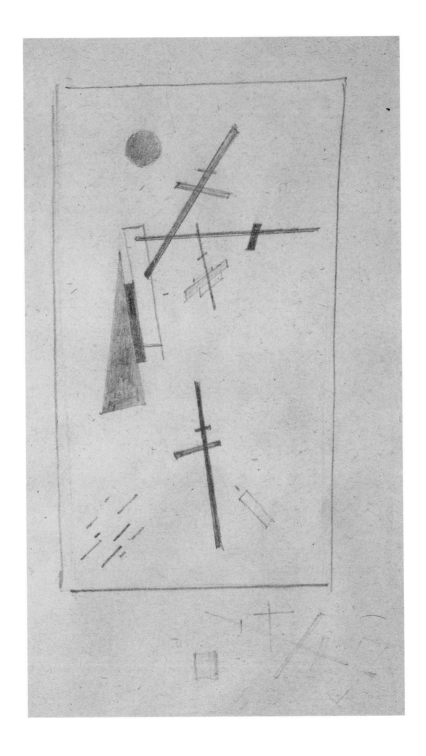

51. Kasimir Malevich (1879-1935), **Suprematist Composition**, c.1916

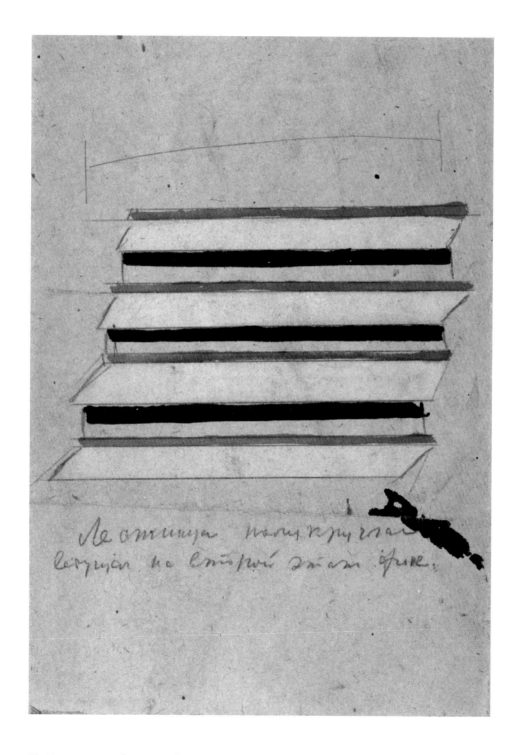

52. Kasimir Malevich (1879-1935), **Steps – Project for Suprematist decor for the Red Theatre Leningrad**, 1931

71. Gerhard Richter (b.1932), **Untitled**, 1986

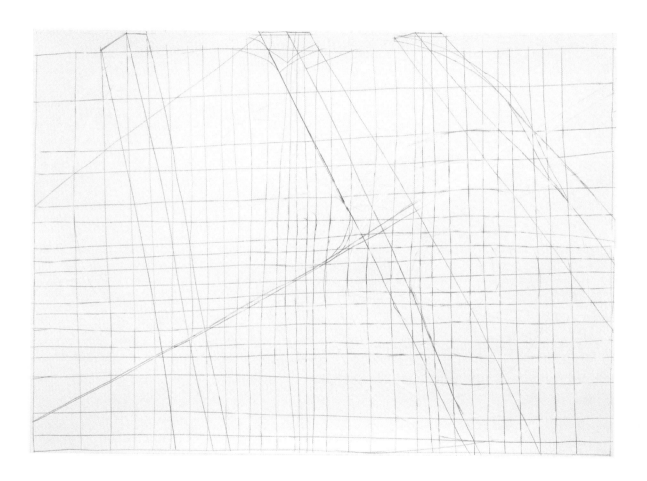

80. German Stegmaier (b.1959), **Untitled**, 2004-2007-2008

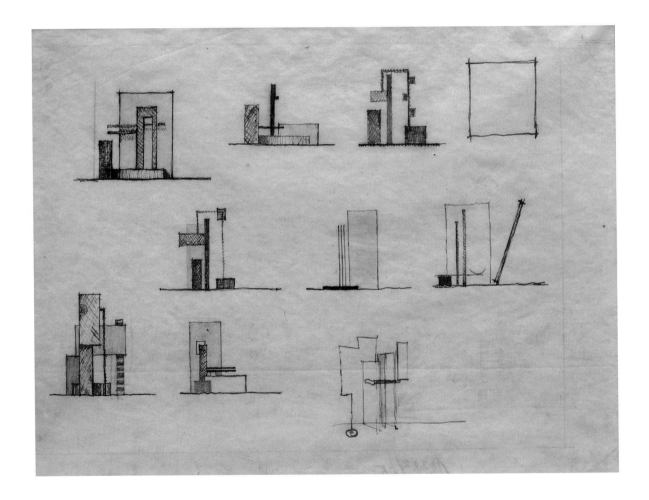

90. Friedrich Vordemberge-Gildewart (1899-1962), **Sketches for architectural project / S22**, 1919

72. Fred Sandback (1943-2003), **Two Aspects of a Two-Part Construction for the Annemarie Verna Gallery, Zürich**, 1976
All works by Fred Sandback © 2010 Fred Sandback Archive

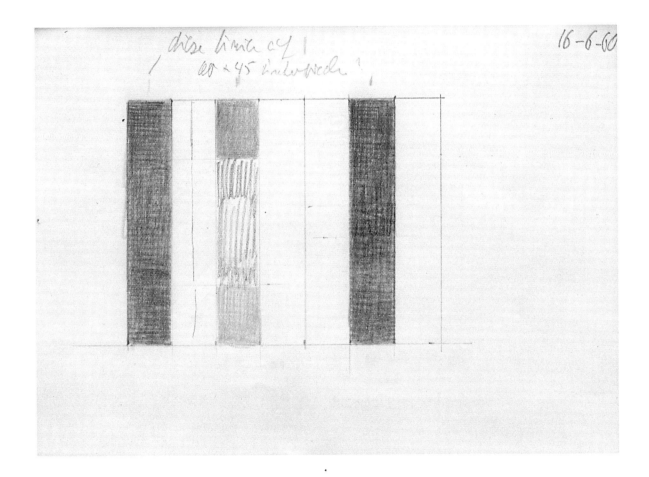

91. Friedrich Vordemberge-Gildewart, **Study for a Composition** / D99, 1960

84. Richard Tuttle (b.1941), **Yellow Verticals**, 1969

88

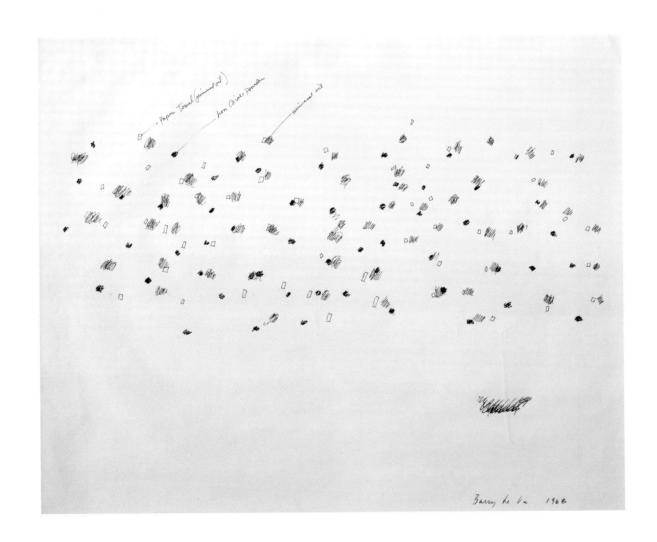

47. Barry Le Va (b.1941), Untitled, 1968

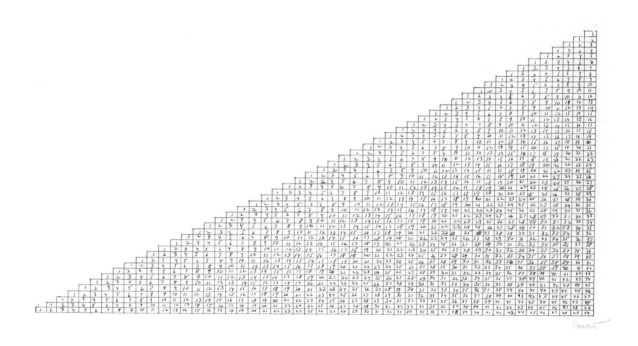

48. Sol LeWitt (1928-2007), **Working Drawing / Concrete Block Structure**, 1996
© ARS, NY and DACS, London 2010

54. Agnes Martin (1912-2004), **Untitled**, 1965

6. James Bishop (b.1927), Untitled, 1970

70. Alan Reynolds (b.1926), **Study – Rotation 5**, 2004

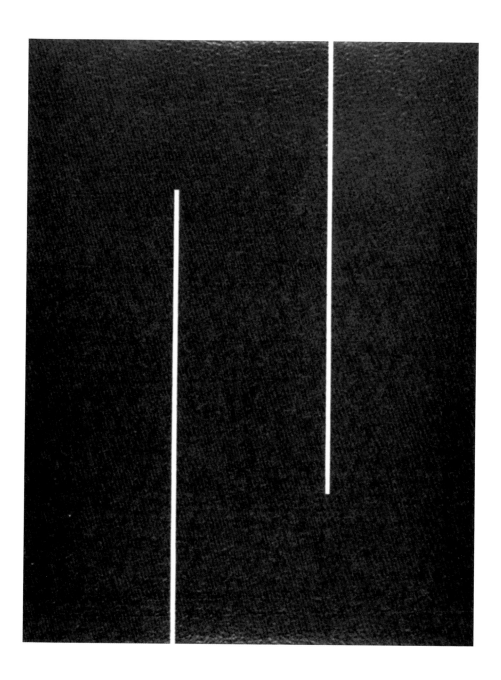

42. Julije Knifer (1924-2004), **Meander**, 1982

34. Katharina Hinsberg (b.1967), **Nulla dies sine linea 4**, 2001

Films

Viking Eggeling (1880-1925)	Diagonalsinfonie (Diagonal Symphony), 1920-24, 7minutes
Hans Richter (1888 -1976)	Rhytmus 21 (Film is Rhythm), 1921, 3.30 minutes
	Filmstudie, 1926, 3.30 minutes
Kasimir Malevich (1879-1935)	Suprematism, 1927/1971, reconstruction, 5 minutes
Fernand Léger (1881-1977)	Le Ballet Mécanique, 1924, sound version, 14 minutes

The former Dadaist painter Hans Richter and the Swedish artist Viking Eggeling met in Berlin in 1919 and decided to collaborate in the making of abstract films, 'absolute films', which would use the cinema screen like a painter's canvas as an illusionary space inhabited by black, grey and white abstract shapes projected upon it. The discovery by the Russian artist Kasimir Malevich of geometric abstraction in 1913 represented for them one of the most liberating acts in modern art. Malevich's Suprematist elements: square, cross, circle, oblong and line, placed on pure white surfaces, seemed to be projected into a world of weightlessness, into infinite space. Richter and Eggeling believed that abstract forms and signs would represent an unexplored 'universal language', like music, capable of communicating emotions and meanings. While developing abstract forms in sequence and rhythmic order, they found visual equivalents to music, echoes of the mathematical shifts in J.S. Bach's system of counterpoint in *Die Kunst der Fuge* (Art of the Fugue).

From 1919 to1924 both Richter and Eggeling created a number of large scroll drawings, of a length varying from 1.50 to 4.40 metres, in which they explored the sequential progression of individual geometric forms and linear complexes. These scrolls were in fact notations, an attempt to systematise the serial representation of abstract forms and a range of formal mutations. While Eggeling drew his first scroll titled *Horizontal-vertikal Messe* (Horizontal-Vertical Mass), which was concentrating on the growth of basic linear elements into complex combinations, Richter based his scrolls *Präludium* (Prelude) and *Fuge* (Fugue) on the interaction of geometric patterns, the dynamics of square and oblong. These conceptual works on paper were to prepare the artists for the next step, to convert motion and time implied in their scroll drawings into 'real' motion, into 'film time'. The first projectable results on screen were some 30 second film strips which Richter incorporated in his first film *Rhytmus* (Film is Rhythm) (1921) and Eggeling included in his long-term project *Diagonalsinfonie* (1920/24).

Theo van Doesburg, the editor of the Dutch magazine *De Stijl*, was the first to draw the attention of the international art community to the work of Richter and Eggeling, describing their advances in the field of the 'absolute film': 'Abstract film did not arrive totally unexpected… The notion of conquering the static character of painting by the dynamic character of film already existed in the minds of many modern artists who have wanted to solve the problems of visual arts with the help of a well-developed film technique, to bring together the dynamic and the static in an aesthetic way.'[1]

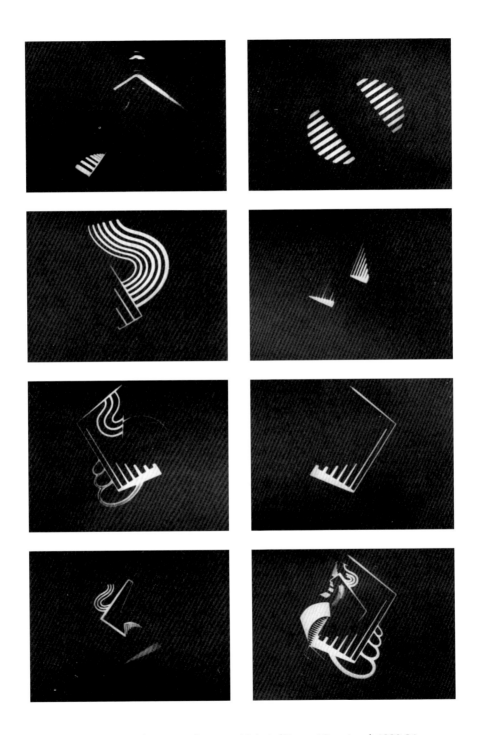

stills from Viking Eggeling (1880-1925), **Diagonalsinfonie (Diagonal Symphony)**, 1920-24

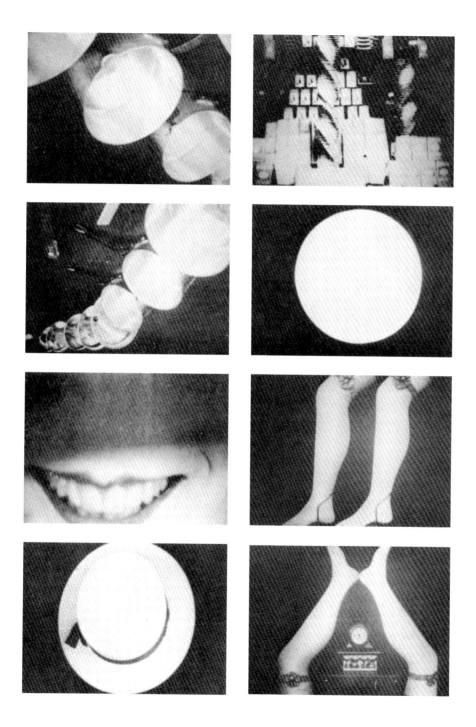

stills from Fernand Léger (1881-1977), Le Ballet Mécanique, 1924

Hans Richter (1888 -1976), design related to **Rhytmus 21 (Film is Rhythm)**, 1921

When Malevich came to Berlin in 1927 he met Richter who showed him a programme of 'absolute films'. These films possessed fluency, a precise sense of timing, clarity and aesthetic validity which impressed the Russian. Finding in Richter an artist who recognised the importance of the Suprematist system and who would be able to devise filmic solutions required for the realisation of his own concept, Malevich felt encouraged to write a scenario for an 'artistic-scientific film' which he dedicated to Hans Richter. Richter intended to collaborate with Malevich in the making of the film, titled *Painting and the Problems of Architecture: The new Classical System of Architecture*, but the project was not realised.

However the next step in experimental artists' films was to belong to *cinéma pur* as first defined in the films and texts of Louis Delluc and Germaine Dulac, who had stated already in 1922 that film had to overcome the phase of realism and 'authentic' emotions, evolving towards the 'visual symphony'.[2] *Cinéma pur* incorporated a sense of sculptural values, the geometric essence and abstractness inherent in close-ups of every-day objects, ideas that surfaced in the films of Man Ray such as *Le retour à la raison* (1923) and in *Entr'acte* (1924) by René Clair and Francis Picabia. Transferring the technique of collage onto film, images, splinters snatched from reality by an omnipotent camera, were treated like *objets trouvés*.

The most influential prototype film of *cinéma pur* was *Ballet Mécanique* (1924), produced by the American film-maker Dudley Murphy in collaboration with Fernand Léger. It was a montage of life action fragments in which the cubist world of objects, seen through prismatic lenses, took over the screen; the switch from positive to negative, short cuts and repeated actions, reversed shots and the smile, the eye, the legs of Kiki de Montparnasse interacted with kitchen implements, wine bottles and Man Ray's straw hat. A score composed by George Antheil synchronised the rhythms of the montage with the syncopations of a Charleston and the noises of the City.

The 'First International Avant-Garde Film Exhibition' took place in Berlin in May 1925. Under the summary title *Der Absolute Film* it brought together examples of *cinéma pur*, including *Ballet Mécanique*, with the films of Eggeling and Richter.[3] During this event clear affinities emerged between the French and German approaches to film-making with regard to subjective experimentation and the common aim to modernise cinema. Futurist notions of simultaneity and speed were eventually combined with the Surrealist poetics of chance. Ideas regarding constructed images as demonstrated in the absolute film were adopted to serve non-narrative films in which images could reveal their formal potential and poetic charge. This new found freedom resulted in films like Richter's *Filmstudie* (1926) and *Vormittagsspuk* (Ghosts Before Breakfast) (1927/28) and Eugen Deslav's *La marche des machines* (1929). Cinematic strategies reached high levels of complexity in the city montages by masters like Alberto Cavalcanti in *Rien que les Heures* (1926) and by Ruttmann and Vertov in *Berlin – Symphony of a City* (1927) and *The Man with the Movie Camera* (1929).

L.B.

footnotes

1   Theo van Doesburg, 'Abstracte Filmbeelding', *De Stijl*, vol.4, no.5, 1921, pp.71-75.

2   Louis Delluc, *Photogenie in Veshch*, No.3, May 1922. and Germaine Dulac, in *L'art cinematographique*, Vol.2, Paris 1927, p.43.

3   Screenings on 3rd and 4th May 1925 at the UFA Palast, Kurfürstendamm, Berlin, were organised jointly by the Novembergruppe and Cultural Department of the UFA film company. Their popular success was seen as a sign of the public readiness to seek out and appreciate works of the film avant-garde.

5. Joseph Beuys (1921-1986), *Painting Version 1-90*, 1976

Drawings

cat. 7

1 **Maliheh Afnan** (b.1935) Iran
Blackboard, 1987
graphite, graphite wash, chalk on paper
50 x 65 cm
Rose Issa Projects, London

2 **William Anastasi** (b.1933) USA
Subway Drawing, 28 November 1967
graphite on paper
19.3 x 29 cm
BM 2007,7075.1
Trustees of the British Museum

3 **Frank Auerbach** (b.1931) Britain
Tree at Tretire, 1975
chalk, charcoal and gouache on two sheets of paper
77 x 72.5 cm
GMA 2848
Scottish National Gallery of Modern Art

4 **Andrés Belmar** (b.1966) Chile
Untitled, 2009
pencil on paper
22 x 18 cm
Galerie Biedermann, Munich

5 **Joseph Beuys** (1921-1986) Germany
Painting Version 1-90, 1976
oil, butter and pigment on paper, torn hole
76 x 56 cm
GMA 4599
Scottish National Gallery of Modern Art ;
purchased with assistance from the National
HeritageMemorial Fund and The Art Fund, 2002

6 **James Bishop** (b.1927) USA
Untitled, 1970
oil and crayon on paper
55.5 x 55.5 cm
AGV Collection

7 **Umberto Boccioni** (1882-1916) Italy
Plastic Dynamism: Horse + Houses, 1914
ink on paper
32 x 41.6 cm
Estorick Collection, London
Kettle's Yard only

8 **David Bomberg** (1890-1957) Britain
Cubist Composition of Figures, c.1912/13
charcoal on paper 50.5 x 69 cm
Circ. 164-1964/FPD 297A
Victoria & Albert Museum

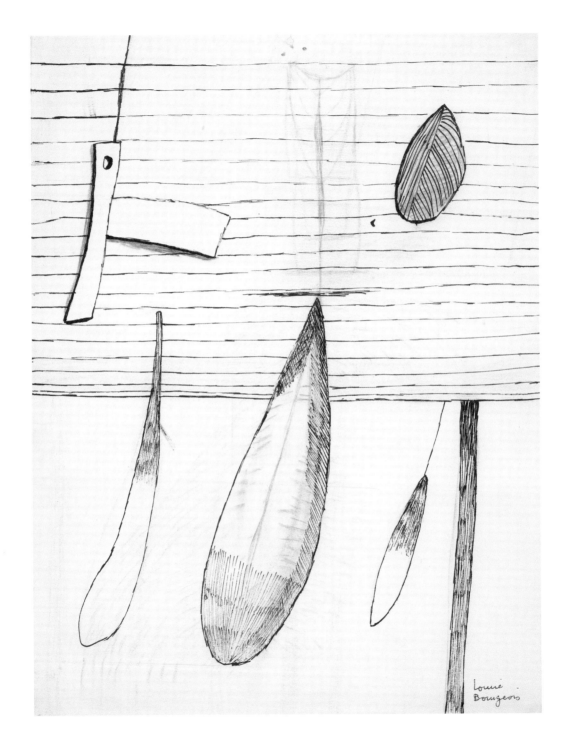

9. Louise Bourgeois (b.1911), **Untitled**, 1947/49
© Louise Bourgeois. DACS, London/VAGA, New York 2010

12 **Carlo Carra** (1881-1966) Italy
Synthesis of a Café Concert, 1910/12
charcoal on paper
75 x 65 cm
Estorick Collection, London
Kettle's Yard only

13 **Carlo Carra** (1881-1966) Italy
Boxer, 1913
ink, charcoal, pencil on paper
44 x 28 cm
Estorick Collection, London
Kettle's Yard only

14 **Patrick Caulfield** (1936-2005) Britain
Study, c.1995
pencil on tracing paper
21 x 17 cm
Private Collection, London

15 **Karel Diericks** (b.1940) Netherlands
Ambrosia, 1999
crayon on paper
36 x 27 cm
Hachmeister Galerie, Münster

9 **Louise Bourgeois** (b.1911) USA
Untitled, 1947/49
ink, charcoal on paper
28.2 x 21.7 cm
BM 1987,0307.11
Trustees of the British Museum

10 **Stuart Brisley** (b.1933) Britain
Pig Wars, 2008
graphite on paper
65 x 104 cm
England and Co.

11 **Karoline Bröckel** (b.1964) Germany
Untitled - Werkgruppe Schnee - Snow, 2006
pencil on paper
71.5 x 101cm
Galerie Werner Klein, Cologne

cat. 15

19. Lyonel Feininger (1871-1956), **Seven Mannikins,** 1954

cat. 24

16   **Otto Dix** (1891-1969)
Klage (Lament), 1915
ink on paper
31.7 x 22.2 cm
Private Collection, New York
Kettle's Yard only

17   **Viking Eggeling** (1880-1925) Sweden
Diagonal Symphony Part IV, 1922/24
pencil on paper scroll
50 x 370 cm
Collection Marion von Hofacker

18   **Jean Fautrier** (1898-1964) France
Sunset, 1964
aquatint and watercolour
49.5 x 54.7 cm
Circ. 441-1964 / MP 295C
Victoria & Albert Museum

19   **Lyonel Feininger** (1871-1956) Germany/USA
Seven Mannikins, 1954
watercolour, crayon, ink on paper
21.7 x 28.9 cm
Marlborough Fine Art

20   **Lothar Fischer** (1933-2004) Germany
Untitled, c1970
ink on paper
43 x 30.5 cm
Galerie Biedermann, Munich

21   **Dan Flavin** (1933-1996) USA
Sailboat, 1986
charcoal on sandpaper
35.5 x 28 cm
AGV Collection

22   **Lucio Fontana** (1899-1968) Italy
Plate one from 'Quattro Litografie', 1955
Lithograph 3/10, hand-coloured
49.7 x 38.8 cm
BM 2005,1030.18.1
Trustees of the British Museum

23   **Naum Gabo** (1890-1977) Russia/USA
Sketch for a Mobile Construction, c1918
drawing on board
33.5 x 26.2 cm
T02155
Tate; presented by the artist, 1977

24   **Henri Gaudier-Brzeska** (1891-1915) France/Britain
Design for a Vorticist Ornament, 1914
crayon on paper
47 x 51.5 cm
Kettle's Yard, University of Cambridge
De La Warr Pavilion only

25   **William Gear** (1915-1997) Britain
Feature in Landscape, 1948
brush, oil on paper
46.3 x 52.7 cm
BM 2003,0601.78
Trustees of the British Museum

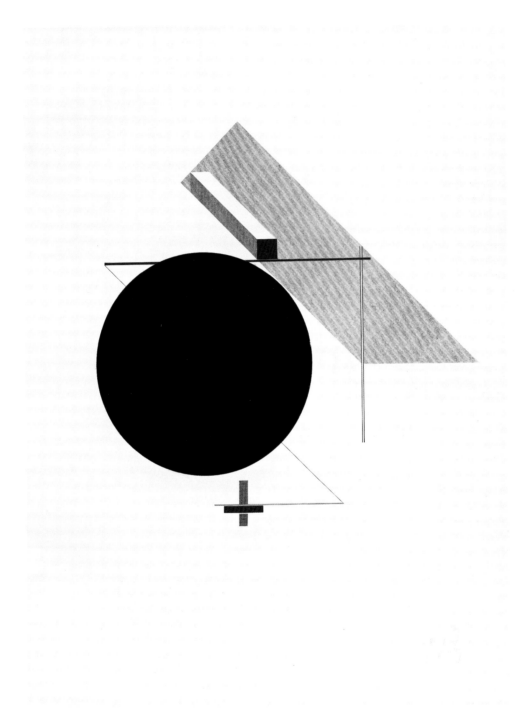

49. El Lissitzky (1890-1941), Proun, 1. Kestnermappe, Hanover, 1923

cat. 28

28 **Michael Goldberg** (1924-2007) USA
Untitled, 2000
mixed media on paper
40 x 26.5 cm
Galerie Biedermann, Munich

29 **Corrado Govoni** (1884-1965) Italy
Self-portrait, 1915
ink on paper
29.5 x 22.5 cm
Estorick Collection, London
Kettle's Yard only

30 **George Grosz** (1893-1959) Germany
War Drawing, 1917
ink on paper
23 x 18.5 cm
Private Collection, New York
Kettle's Yard only

31 **Philip Guston** (1913-1980) USA
Hooded, 1968
charcoal on paper
40.5 x 58.6 cm
BM 2004,0601.20
Trustees of the British Museum

32 **Susan Hefuna,** (b. 1962) Egypt/Germany
Building, 2009
ink on paper and overlaid tracing paper
51 x 78 cm
Rose Issa Projects, London

33 **Barbara Hepworth** (1903-1975) Britain
St. Rémy, Provence, 1933
pencil on paper
31 x 37.8 cm
Private Collection

34 **Katharina Hinsberg** (b.1967) Germany
Nulla dies sine linea 4, 2001
paper cube, ink, pen on 931 + 269 single
sheets
21 x 21 x 21 cm
Private Collection, Neuss
Courtesy Galerie Werner Klein, Cologne

26 **Alberto Giacometti** (1901-1966) Switzerland
The Skull, 1923
pencil on paper
29.9 x 21.6 cm
UEA 59
Robert and Lisa Sainsbury Collection,
University of East Anglia

27 **Raimund Girke** (1930-2002) Germany
Untitled, 1998
pencil on paper
27 x 30cm
Galerie Werner Klein, Cologne

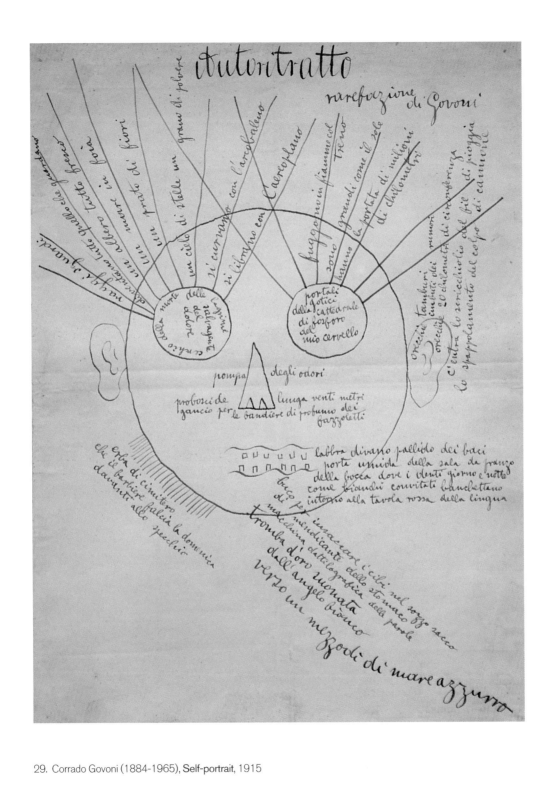

29. Corrado Govoni (1884-1965), Self-portrait, 1915

cat. 39 © DACS 2010

35 **Katharina Hinsberg**
Untitled, Lines / Grid, 2009
coloured pencil on paper, cut out
59.5 x 49.5cm
Galerie Werner Klein, Cologne

36 **Rachel Howard** (b.1969) Britain
Untitled Drawing 5, 2007
brush, ink on paper
56 x 75.5 cm
Courtesy Murderme

37 **Donald Judd** (1928-1994) USA
Untitled, 1978
graphite on paper
55.8 x 76.2 cm
AGV Collection

38 **Linda Karshan** (b.1947) USA/Britain
Untitled, 25.06.1998
76 x 56 cm
graphite on paper
The artist
Courtesy Redfern Gallery, London

39 **Paul Klee** (1879-1940) Switzerland
Old Man Counting, 1929
etching
29.9 x 23.9 cm
BM 1930,0118.13
Trustees of the British Museum

40 **Franz Kline** (1910-1962) USA
Untitled, 1957/58
brush, ink on paper
21.5 x 27 9 cm
BM 1977,0611.4
Trustees of the British Museum

41 **Gustav Klucis** (1895-1938) Latvia
Architectural Study, 1921/22
gouache, ink and pencil on paper laid on card
39.5 x 24.8 cm
Annely Juda Fine Art Ltd, London

42 **Julije Knifer** (1924-2004) Croatia
Meander, 1982
graphite on paper
65 x 50 cm
Zivojin and Ingrid Dacić

43 **Willem de Kooning** (1904-1997) USA
Figure in a Landscape, c.1970/75
charcoal on paper
27.6 x 21.2 cm
BM 2004,0601.10
Trustees of the British Museum

44 **Willem de Kooning**
Untitled, 1966/67
charcoal on tracing paper
47.6 x 61 cm
T01104
Tate: presented by the artist through the
American Federation of Arts, 1969

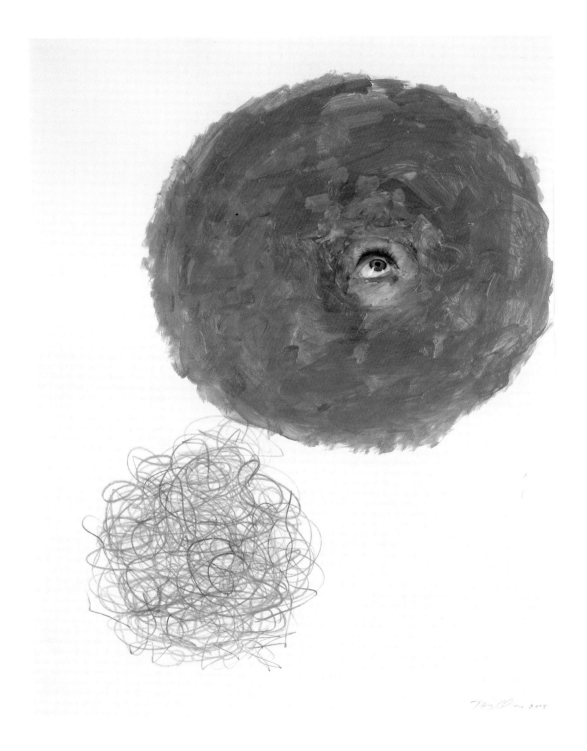

64. Tony Oursler (b.1957), Eye, 2005

cat. 53 © DACS 2010

45 **Michail Larionov** (1881-1964) Russia
White Drawing, ?1907
gouache, pencil on paper
22.9 x 34 cm
T00175
Tate

46 **Fernand Léger** (1881-1977) France
Trees, 1923
pencil on paper
32.5 x 24.5 cm
T06807
Tate; bequeathed by Elly Kahnweiler, 1991

47 **Barry Le Va** (b.1941) USA
Untitled, 1968
ink on paper
47 x 59.5 cm
Private Collection, New York
Kettle's Yard only

48 **Sol LeWitt** (1928-2007) USA
Working Drawing / Concrete Block Structure, 1996
ink on paper
33.4 x 61 cm
Estate of Sol LeWitt
Courtesy Annemarie Verna Galerie, Zürich

49 **El Lissitzky** (1890-1941) Russia
Kestnermappe Proun /
Proun. 1st Kestner Portfolio, Hanover, 1923
six lithographs (two with collage),
including cover and title page, 60 x 44 cm
GMA 2767
Scottish National Gallery of Modern Art

50 **Lucebert (Lubertus J. Swaanswijk)**
(1924-1994) Netherlands
Untitled, 1962
ink on paper
26 x 20 cm
Private Collection, London

51 **Kasimir Malevich** (1879-1935) Russia
Suprematist Composition, c.1916
pencil on paper
18.2 x 11 cm
Annely Juda Fine Art Ltd, London

66. Eduardo Paolozzi, **Collage**, 1953
© Trustees of the Paolozzi Foundation, Licensed by DACS 2010

52   **Kasimir Malevich**
Steps - Project for Suprematist decor
for the Red Theatre Leningrad, 1931
watercolour and pencil on paper
21.4 x 15 cm
Annely Juda Fine Art Ltd, London

53   **Piero Manzoni** (1933-1963) Italy
Line 4.9m, December 1959
ink on paper with cardboard container
22.2 x 6.3 x 6.3 cm
T01874.002
Tate

54   **Agnes Martin** (1912-2004) USA
Untitled, 1965
ink on paper
22.3 x 22.3 cm
AGV Collection

55   **Kenneth Martin** (1905-1984) Britain
Drawing for Screw Mobile, 1967
pencil and crayon on paper
76.8 x 55.9 cm
Annely Juda Fine Art Ltd, London

56   **Henri Michaux** (1899-1984) France
Composition c1960-1962
ink on paper
75.5 x 104 cm
AGV Collection

57   **Joan Mitchell** (1926-1992) USA
Untitled, 1959/60
screen-print, unique printer's proof
44.3 x 37.1 cm
BM 1995,0402.2
Trustees of the British Museum

58   **Piet Mondrian** (1872-1944) Netherlands
Tree Study, early 1913
graphite on paper
12.4 x 17.6 cm
BM 1980,0628.9
Trustees of the British Museum

59   **Robert Motherwell** (1915-1991) USA
In Black and White, 1960
gouache and pencil on paper
58.1 x 73.6 cm
GMA 1081
Scottish National Gallery of Modern Art

60   **Zoran Music** (1909-2005) Italy
Four heads with curly hair, 1973
pastel on paper
38 x 56 cm
UEA 1069
Robert and Lisa Sainsbury Collection,
University of East Anglia

61   **Ben Nicholson** (1894-1982) Britain
St. Rémy, Provence, 1933
pencil on paper
30.5 x 37.4 cm
Private Collection

62   **Ben Nicholson**
Drawing (Version 2), 1936
pencil on paper with gesso ground
38.2 x 29.2 cm
Private Collection

63   **Claes Oldenburg** (b. 1929) USA
The Colossal Soap seen from the Riverbank
in Moonlight-Going, 1991
charcoal on paper
63.5 x 99.1 cm
Galerie Biedermann, Munich
Kettle's Yard only

64   **Tony Oursler** (b.1957) USA
Untitled/Eye, 2005
acrylic, chalk, collage on paper
35.5 x 27.9 cm
Galerie Biedermann, Munich

65   **Eduardo Paolozzi** (1924-2005) Britain
London Zoo Aquarium, 1951
ink and watercolour on paper
56.2 x 76.2 cm
GMA 4023
Scottish National Gallery of Modern Art ;
bequesthed by Gabrielle Keiller, 1995

74. Kurt Schwitters, *Big Fight*, 1947
© DACS 2010

cat. 59 © Dedalus Foundation, Inc./DACS, London/VAGA, New York 2010

66 **Eduardo Paolozzi**
Collage, 1953
silk-screen, gouache, ink on paper
53.5 x 69 cm
GMA 4026
Scottish National Gallery of Modern Art;
bequeathed by Gabrielle Keiller, 1995

67 **Jackson Pollock** (1912-1956) USA
Untitled, 1951
ink and gouache on paper
63.1 x 99.9 cm
GMA 849
Scottish National Gallery of Modern Art

68 **Liubov Popova** (1889-1924) Russia
Spatial Force Construction 1921
ink and gouache on paper
34.5 x 27 cm
Galerie Alex Lachmann, Cologne

69 **David Rabinowitch** (b.1943) USA
Construction of Vision
(2 colour properties, 2 tangents) VIII, 1973
pencil and coloured pencil on paper
76 x 57 cm
The artist
Courtesy Annemarie Verna Galerie, Zürich

70 **Alan Reynolds** (b.1926) Britain
Study – Rotation 5, 2004
pencil on paper laid on card
40.6 x 40.6 cm
Annely Juda Fine Art Ltd, London

71 **Gerhard Richter** (b.1932) Germany
26.5.86 (no) 1, 1986
graphite on paper
29.7 x 21 cm
BM 1987,1003.30
Trustees of the British Museum

72 **Fred Sandback** (1943-2003) USA
Two Aspects of a Two-Part Construction
for the Annemarie Verna Gallery, Zürich, 1976
pencil and coloured chalk on paper
76.5 x 57.5 cm
AGV Collection

73 **Kurt Schwitters** (1887-1948) Germany
Koi, 1932
collage, overprint
15.7 x 12.5 cm
T12395
Tate; accepted by H.M. Government in lieu of
Inheritance Tax and allocated to Tate, 2007

74 **Kurt Schwitters**
Big Fight, 1947
collage
17.8 x 11.5 cm
RWS. 62 L/P.7-1978
Victoria & Albert Museum

75 **Richard Serra** (b.1939) USA
Weight and Measure, 1993
etching
171 x 79.5 cm
P20144
Tate; presented by the artist, 1994

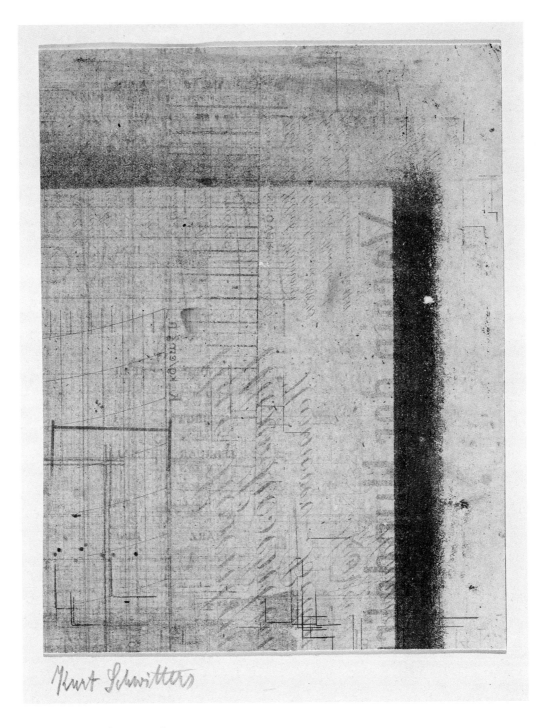

73. Kurt Schwitters (1887-1948), Koi, 1932
© DACS 2010

cat. 82

76 **Richard Serra**
Tracks # 46, 2008
paint-stick on handmade paper
101.6 x 101.6 cm
Gagosian Gallery, London

77 **Joel Shapiro** (b.1941) USA
Untitled, 1994
pencil, charcoal and gouache
68.3 x 41.3 cm
Galerie Biedermann, Munich
Kettle's Yard only

78 **Kurt Sonderborg** (1923-2008) Denmark/Germany
Untitled, 1962
ink on paper
32.7 x 25 cm
BM 1986,1108.5
Trustees of the British Museum

79 **Louis Soutter** (1871-1942) Switzerland
Errant toujours, les Juifs
(Always wandering, the Jews), 1930/37
ink on paper
34 x 49.5 cm
Hachmeister Galerie, Münster

80 **German Stegmaier** (b.1959) Germany
Untitled, 2004-2007-2008
pencil on paper
25.6 x 36.2 cm
Galerie Werner Klein, Cologne

81 **Friedemann von Stockhausen** (b.1945) Germany
Head, 1988
charcoal on paper
62 x 48.3 cm
The artist

82 **Franciszka Themerson** (1907-1988) Poland/Britain
Untitled, 1972
ink, wash, collage on paper
61.5 x 36.5 cm
Private Collection, London

83 **Mark Tobey** (1890-1976) USA
Night Celebration III, 1971
Tempera on black card
45 x 60 cm
Heiner Hachmeister, Münster

84 **Richard Tuttle** (b.1941) USA
Yellow Verticals, 1969
pencil and coloured pencil on paper
30.5 x 22.8 cm
AGV Collection

92. Edward Wadsworth (1889-1949), **Abstract Composition**, 1915

cat. 94

85 **Cy Twombly** (b. 1928) USA
Untitled, 1971
white chalk on grey paper
71 x 100 cm
Private Collection

86 **Nadezhda Udaltsova** (1886-1961) Russia
Composition, 1916
pencil and gouache on paper
41 x 30 cm
Galerie Alex Lachmann, Cologne

87 **Georges Vantongerloo** (1886-1965) Netherlands
Sketches, c.1936/37
pencil and gouache on paper
27 x 21 cm
Annely Juda Fine Art Ltd, London

88 **Emilio Vedova** (1919-2006) Italy
'No, No, No', 1969
lithograph, proof reworked by the artist
50 x 40 cm
BM 2005.4.29.1
Trustees of the British Museum

89 **Emilio Vedova**
Untitled, 1989
relief print on paper
107.5 x 142.4 cm
P11272
Tate; presented by
Garner H. Tullis and Pamela Auchincloss, 1990

90 **Friedrich Vordemberge-Gildewart**
(1899-1962) Germany
Sketches for architectural project / S22, 1919
ink and pencil on paper
25.2 x 36.2 cm
Annely Juda Fine Art Ltd, London

91 **Friedrich Vordemberge-Gildewart**
Study for a Composition / D99, 1960
crayon on paper
14.7 x 21 cm
Annely Juda Fine Art Ltd, London

92 **Edward Wadsworth** (1889-1949) Britain
Abstract Composition, 1915
gouache, pen, pencil on paper
41.9 x 34.3 cm
T00109
Tate

93 **Andor Weininger** (1899-1986) Hungary
Ballerina, 1926
pencil, watercolour on squared-up paper
19 x 12 cm
Inv.18688c
Theaterwissenschaftliche Sammlung,
University of Cologne

94 **Victor Willing** (1928-1987) Britain
Untitled 12.4.80, 1980
charcoal and pastel
26 x 28 cm
Collection Cas Willing

Acknowledgements

Grant-aid by The Isaac Newton Trust of Trinity College enabled the appointment of Lutz Becker as the first Kettle's Yard Curatorial Fellow. An Arts Council England Grant for the Arts supported the realisation of the exhibition. The Museums, Libraries and Archives Council has helped us once again by providing cover for loans under the Government Indemnity scheme.

We are grateful for the enormous generosity of artists and owners, both public and private, who have lent works. In particular we would like to thank our colleagues in national museums who provided the foundation stones of the exhibition: Antony Griffiths, Stephen Coppel and Janice Reading at The British Museum, Caroline Collier, Matthew Gale and Nicole Simões da Silva at Tate, Patrick Elliott, Daniel Herrmann and Janice Slater at the Scottish National Gallery of Modern Art, and Julius Bryant and Peter Ellis at the V&A. Our thanks also go to Jane Bhoyroo and Niki Braithwaite at Arts Council England East and Maxyne McDonald at the MLA.

The exhibition is the work of Lutz Becker who courageously took on a daunting brief and has produced this remarkable anthology. We thank him warmly and he, in turn, would like to add his thanks to his co-authors, Nick Wadley, David Elliott and Iain Boyd Whyte, and to Gilla Bertotti, Richard Hollis, Iraida Icaza, Howard Karshan, Arlette Kunz, Pablo Ventura, Felix von Moreau, Bob White and Oliver Wicks.

MH / AH

LOTTERY FUNDED

Lenders

AGV Collection, Zürich 6, 21, 37, 54, 56, 72, 84

Galerie Biedermann, Munich 4, 20, 28, 63, 64, 77

Trustees of the British Museum
2, 9, 22, 25, 31, 39, 40, 43, 57, 58, 59, 71, 78, 88

Ingrid and Zivojin Dacić 42

England & Co. 10

Estorick Collection, London 7, 12, 13, 29

Gagosian Gallery, London 76

Hachmeister Galerie, Münster 15, 79

Heiner Hachmeister, Münster 83

Collection Marion von Hofacker 17

Rose Issa Projects, London 1, 32

Annely Juda Fine Art Ltd, London 41, 51, 52, 55, 70, 87, 90, 91

Linda Karshan, courtesy Redfern Gallery 38

Kettle's Yard, University of Cambridge 24

Galerie Werner Klein, Cologne 11, 27, 35, 80

Galerie Alex Lachmann, Cologne 68, 86

Estate of Sol LeWitt, courtesy Annemarie Verna Galerie, Zürich 48

Marlborough Fine Art 19

Murderme 36

David Rabinowitch, courtesy Annemarie Verna Galerie, Zürich 69

Robert and Lisa Sainsbury Collection, University of East Anglia 26, 60

Scottish National Gallery of Modern Art 3, 5, 49, 65, 66, 67

Friedemann von Stockhausen 81

Tate 23, 44, 45, 46, 53, 73, 75, 89, 92

Theaterwisserschaftliche Sammlung, University of Cologne 93

Victoria & Albert Museum, London 8, 18, 74

Cas Willing 94

Private Collection, Neuss, courtesy Galerie Werner Klein, Cologne 34

Private Collections 14, 16, 30, 33, 47, 50, 61, 62, 82, 85